This Notebook Is Mine

_____

Signed

This is a Notebook specifically designed for stand-up comedians, Comedy writers, Comedy Students, Sketch Writers, Advertising Slogan Creators, Copywriters, Playwrights, Tv writers and basically anybody who wants to incorporate humor and Jokes in their work.

This book is separated into Eight Sections

1. Idea 1 - Space to incorporate an Idea

2. Idea 2 - Space to incorporate another Idea

3. Connections - An area to check how these two ideas can intersect

For example, Idea 1 can be Parking Space and Idea 2 can be How men view sex

We could start comparing Parking Space to Sex. 1. How men are looking for a convenient parking space all the time 2. How men want to check if they can get into a parking space even if a parking space is occupied and so on

4. Related Topics to the Joke

5. Additional Puns

6. Characters

7. Set up for the jokes

8. Punch lines for the joke

We have ensured that the size of the book is quite large so that there is sufficient space to scribble all around.

Brainstorming

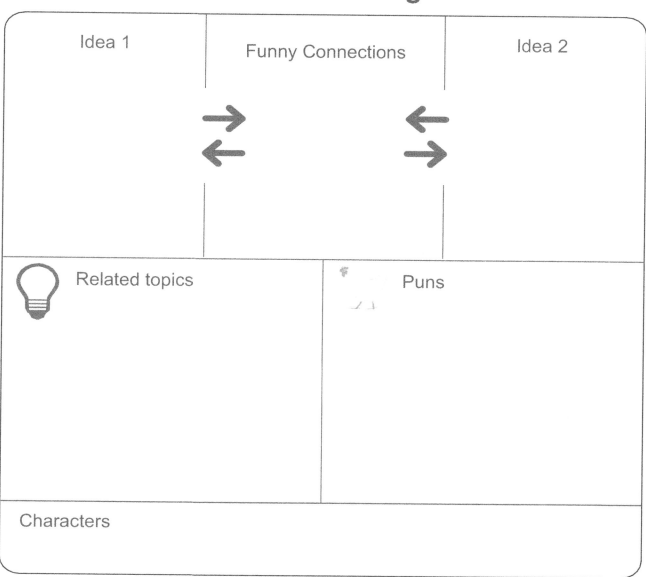

Idea 1	Funny Connections	Idea 2

Related topics

Puns

Characters

Joke

Setup

Punchline

Brainstorming

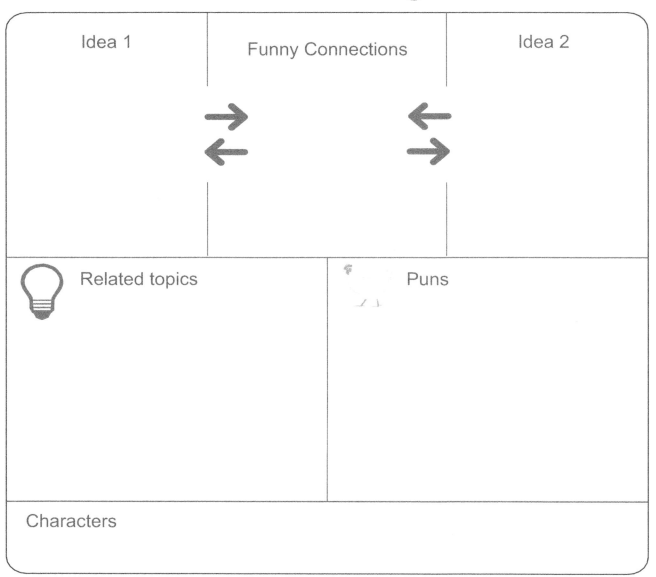

Idea 1	Funny Connections	Idea 2

Related topics

Puns

Characters

Joke

Setup

Punchline

Brainstorming

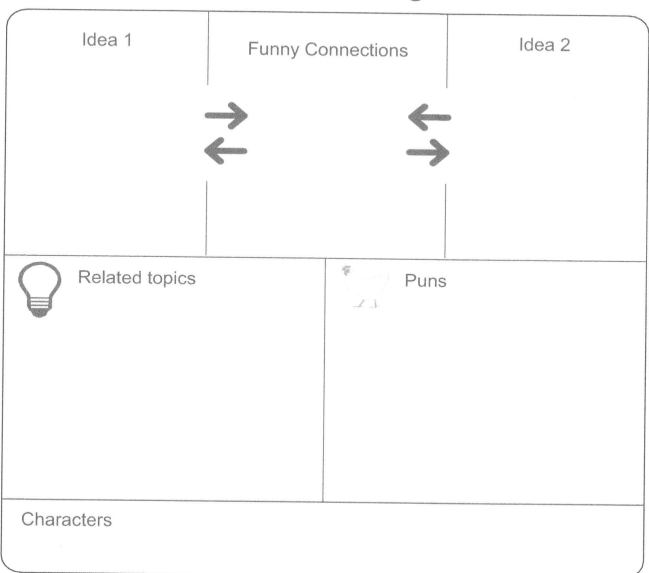

Idea 1	Funny Connections	Idea 2

Related topics

Puns

Characters

Joke

Setup

Punchline

Brainstorming

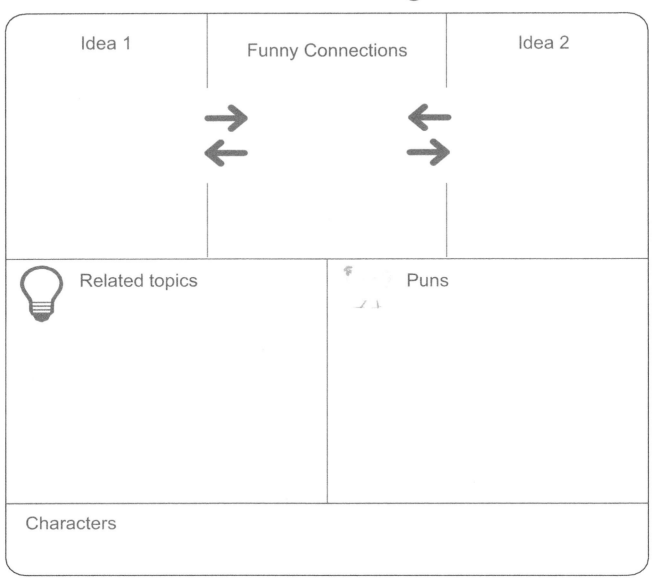

Idea 1	Funny Connections	Idea 2

Related topics

Puns

Characters

Joke

Setup

Punchline

Brainstorming

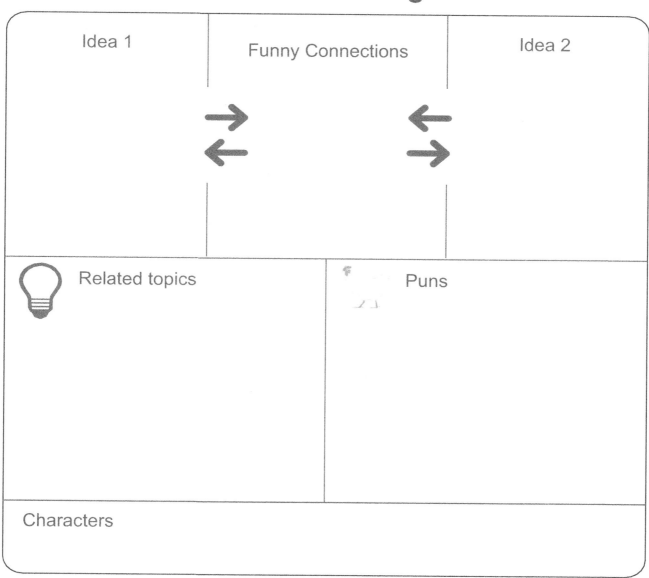

Idea 1	Funny Connections	Idea 2

💡 Related topics	Puns

Characters

Joke

Setup

Punchline

Brainstorming

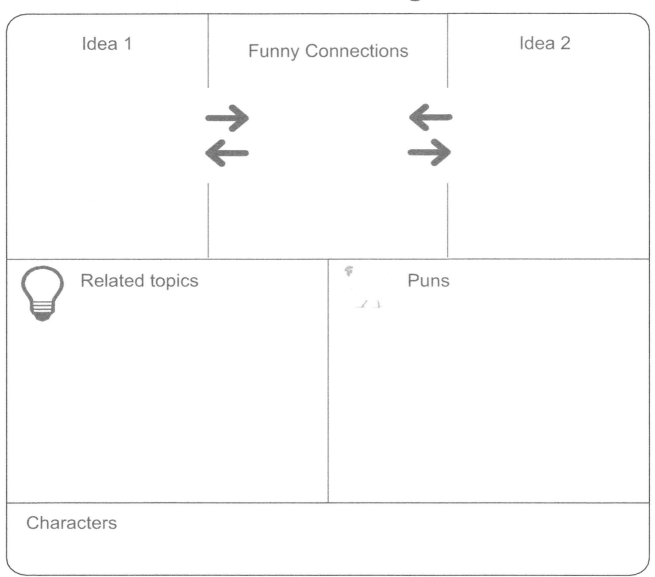

Idea 1	Funny Connections	Idea 2

Related topics

Puns

Characters

Joke

Setup

Punchline

Brainstorming

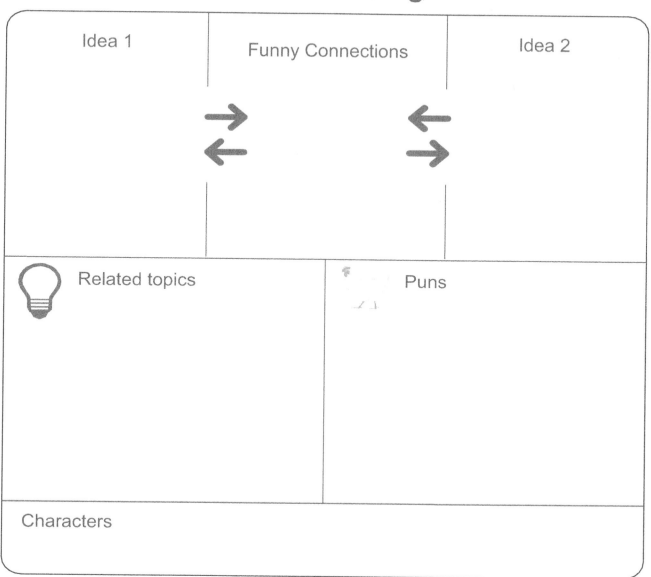

Idea 1	Funny Connections	Idea 2

Related topics

Puns

Characters

Joke

Setup

Punchline

Brainstorming

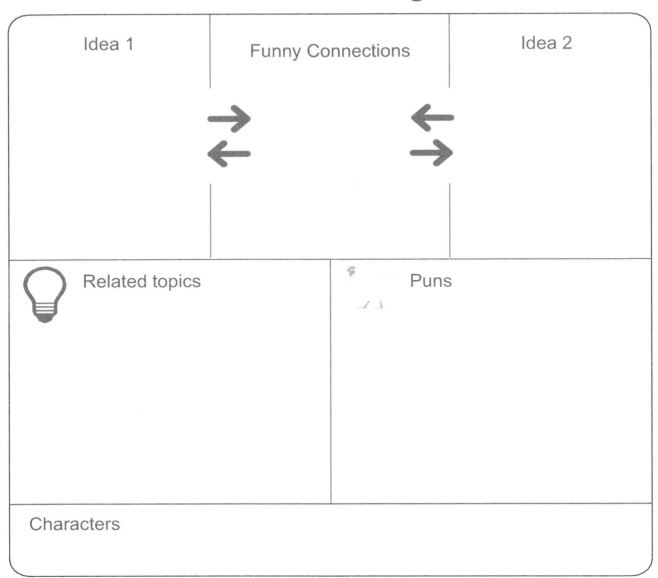

Idea 1	Funny Connections	Idea 2

Related topics

Puns

Characters

Joke

Setup

Punchline

Brainstorming

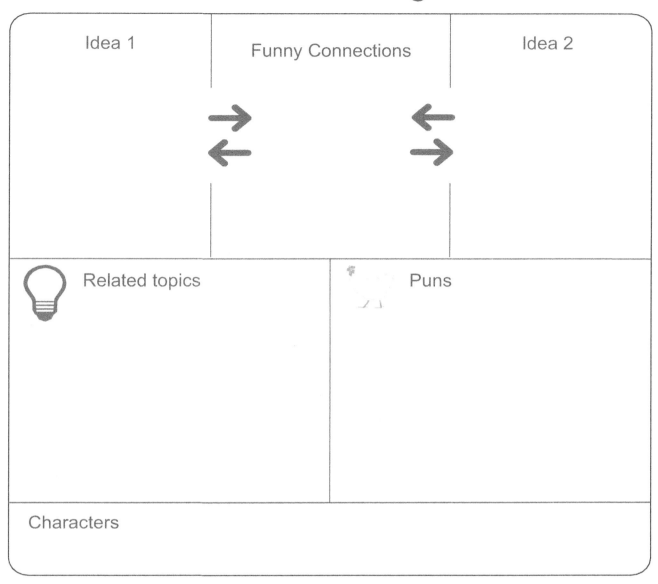

Idea 1	Funny Connections	Idea 2

Related topics

Puns

Characters

Joke

Setup

Punchline

Brainstorming

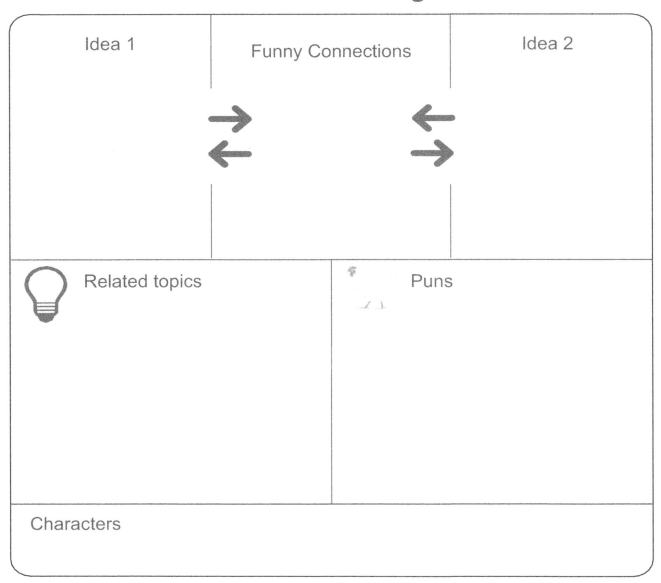

Idea 1	Funny Connections	Idea 2

Related topics

Puns

Characters

Joke

Setup

Punchline

Brainstorming

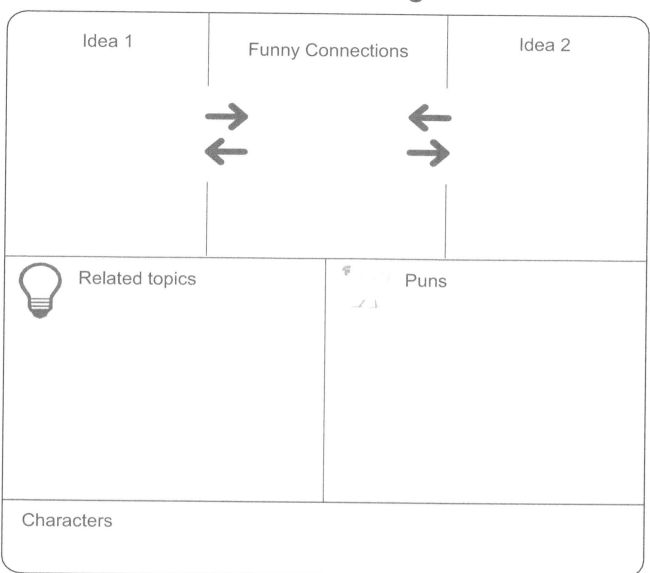

Idea 1	Funny Connections	Idea 2

Related topics

Puns

Characters

Joke

Setup

Punchline

Brainstorming

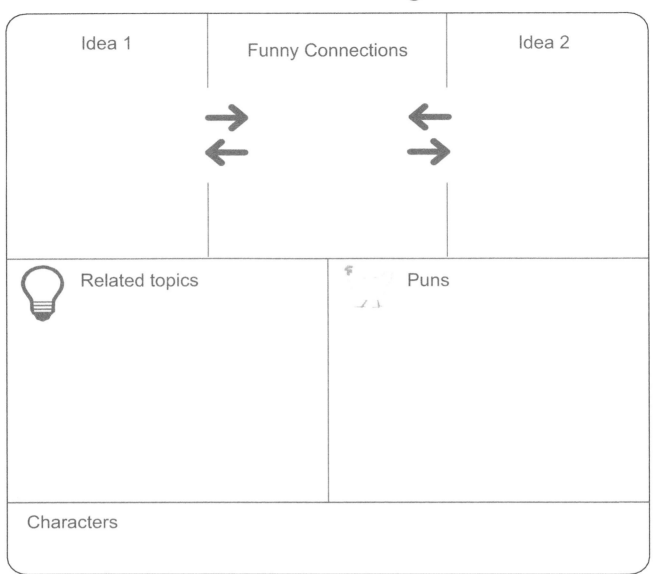

Idea 1	Funny Connections	Idea 2

Related topics

Puns

Characters

Joke

Setup

Punchline

Brainstorming

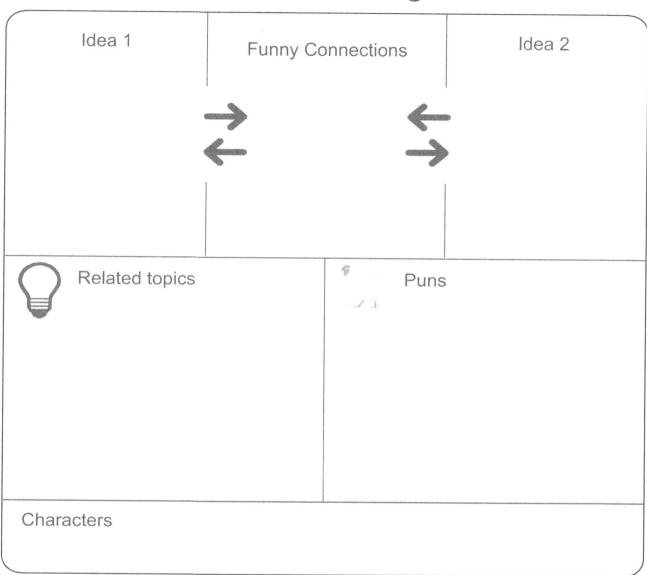

Idea 1	Funny Connections	Idea 2

Related topics

Puns

Characters

Joke

Setup

Punchline

Brainstorming

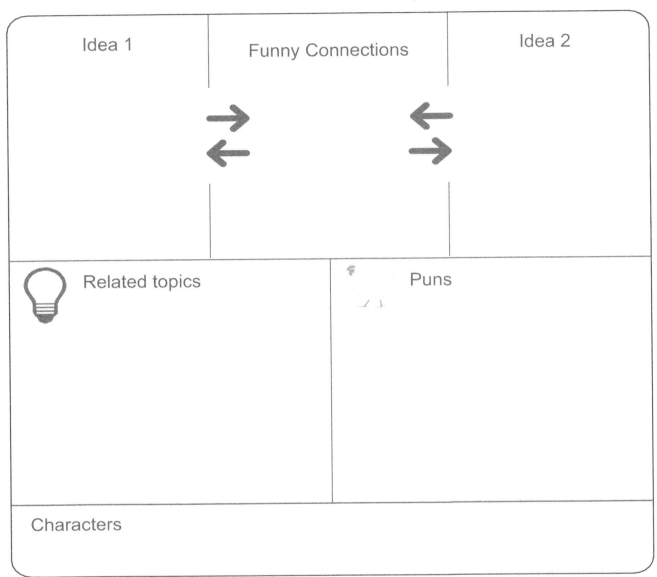

Idea 1	Funny Connections	Idea 2

Related topics

Puns

Characters

Joke

Setup

Punchline

Brainstorming

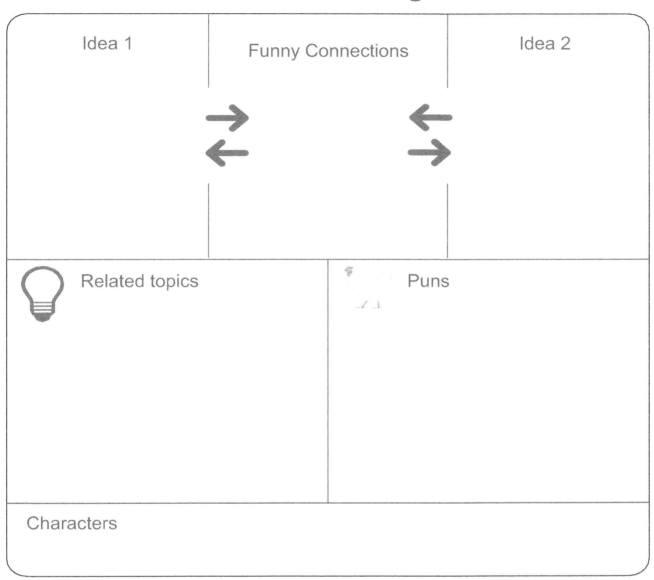

Idea 1	Funny Connections	Idea 2

Related topics

Puns

Characters

Joke

Setup

Punchline

Brainstorming

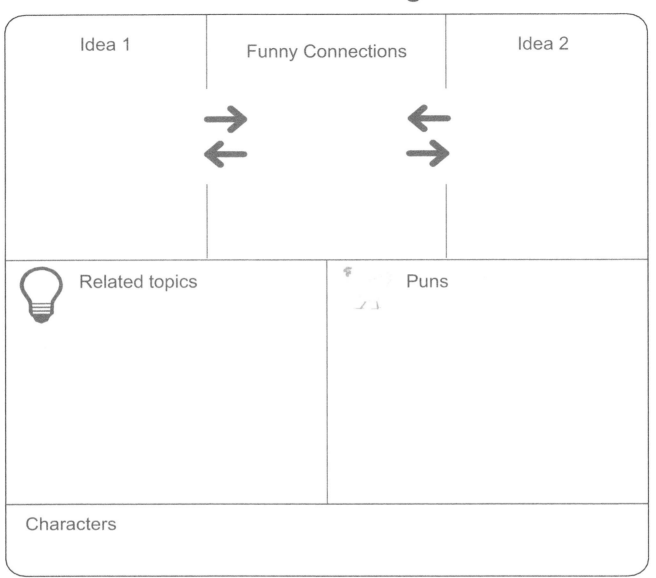

Idea 1	Funny Connections	Idea 2

Related topics

Puns

Characters

Joke

Setup

Punchline

Brainstorming

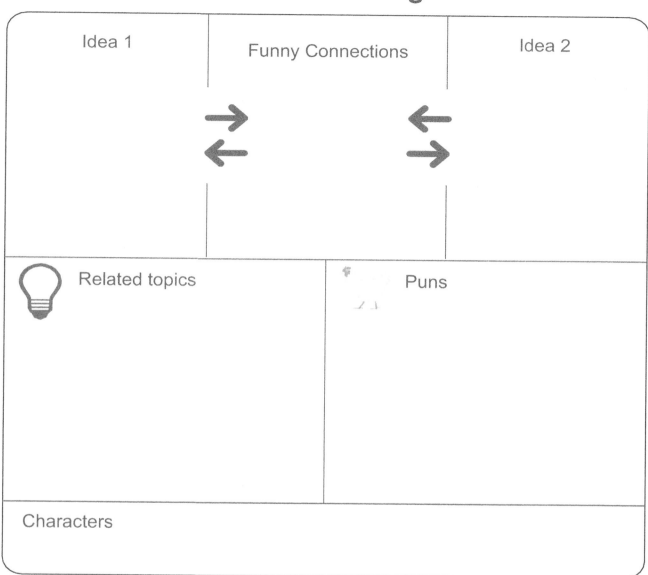

Idea 1	Funny Connections	Idea 2

Related topics	Puns

Characters

Joke

Setup

Punchline

Brainstorming

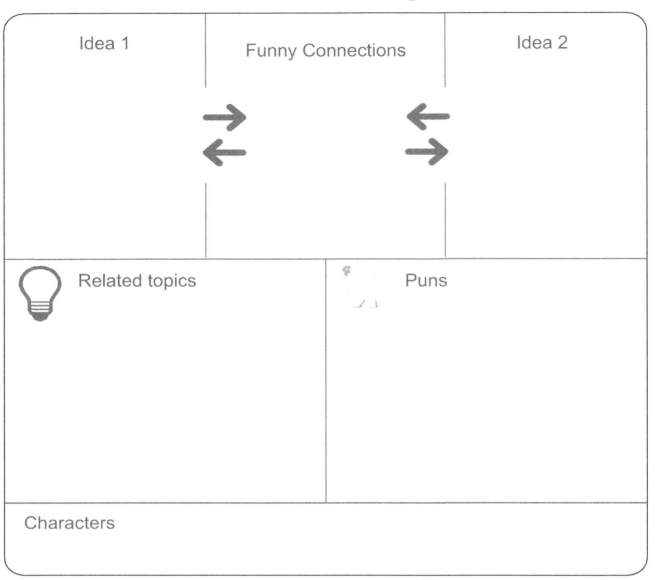

Idea 1	Funny Connections	Idea 2

💡 Related topics

Puns

Characters

Joke

Setup

Punchline

Brainstorming

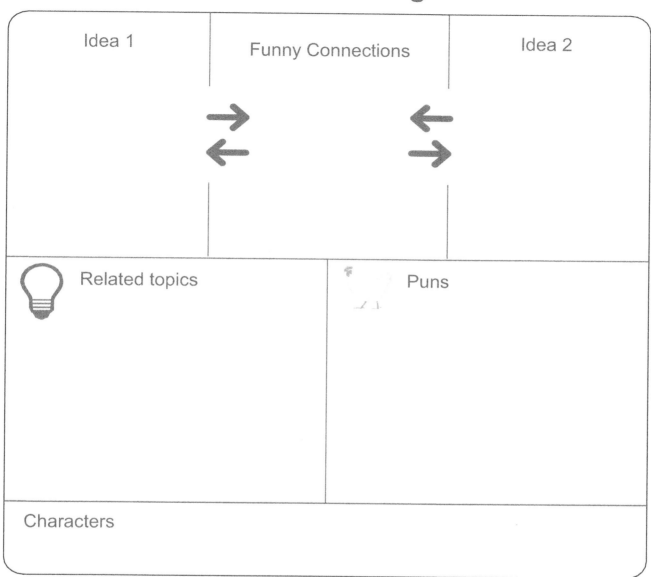

Idea 1	Funny Connections	Idea 2

Related topics

Puns

Characters

Joke

Setup

Punchline

Brainstorming

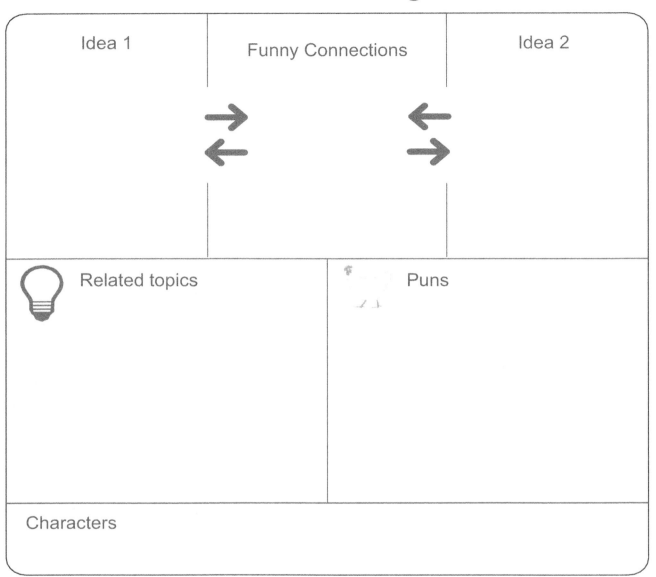

Idea 1	Funny Connections	Idea 2

Related topics

Puns

Characters

Joke

Setup

Punchline

Brainstorming

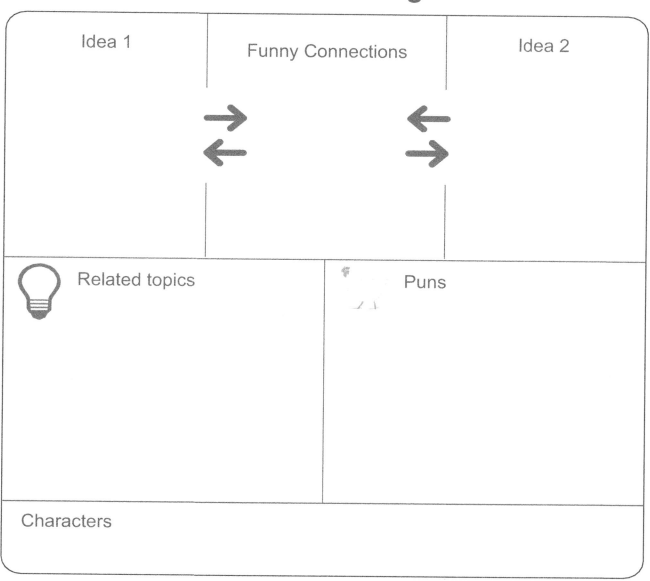

Idea 1	Funny Connections	Idea 2

Related topics

Puns

Characters

Joke

Setup

Punchline

Brainstorming

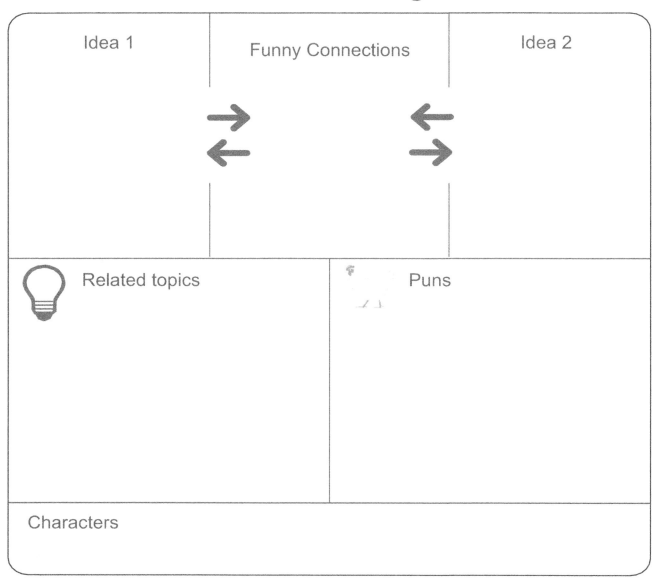

Idea 1	Funny Connections	Idea 2

Related topics

Puns

Characters

Joke

Setup

Punchline

Brainstorming

Idea 1	Funny Connections	Idea 2

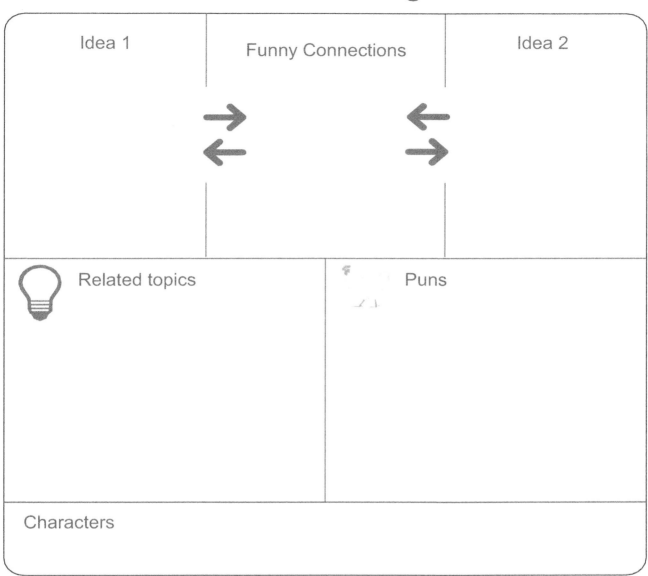

Related topics

Puns

Characters

Joke

Setup

Punchline

Brainstorming

Idea 1	Funny Connections	Idea 2

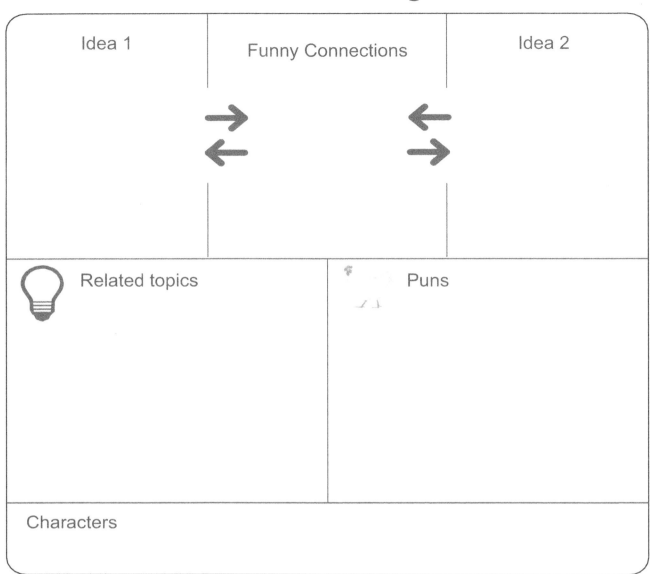

Related topics

Puns

Characters

Joke

Setup

Punchline

Brainstorming

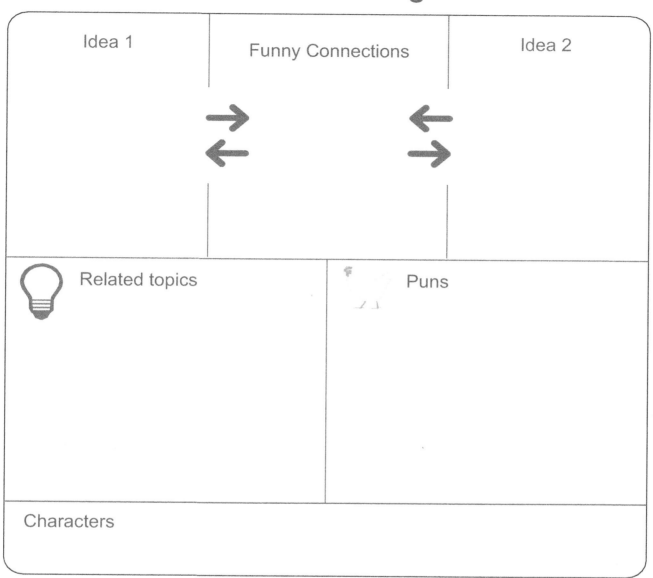

Idea 1	Funny Connections	Idea 2

Related topics

Puns

Characters

Joke

Setup

Punchline

Brainstorming

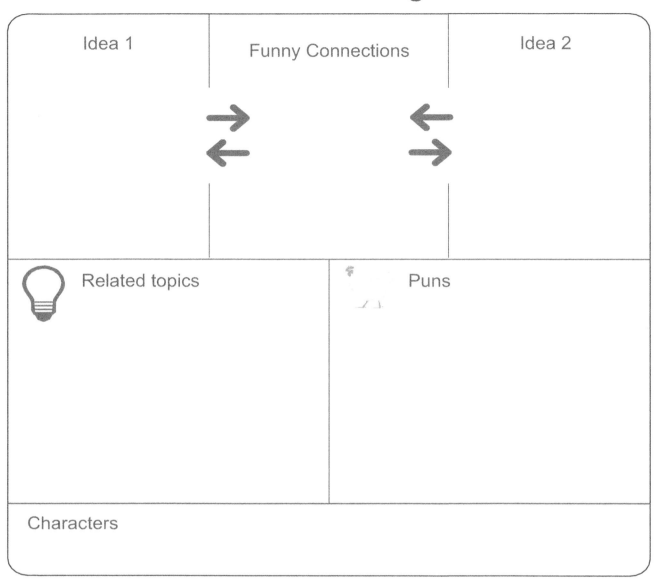

Idea 1	Funny Connections	Idea 2

Related topics

Puns

Characters

Joke

Setup

Punchline

Brainstorming

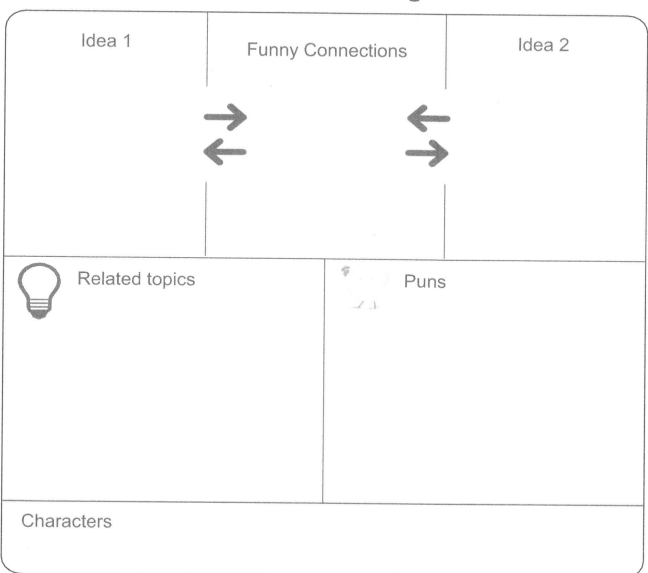

Idea 1

Funny Connections

Idea 2

Related topics

Puns

Characters

Joke

Setup

Punchline

Brainstorming

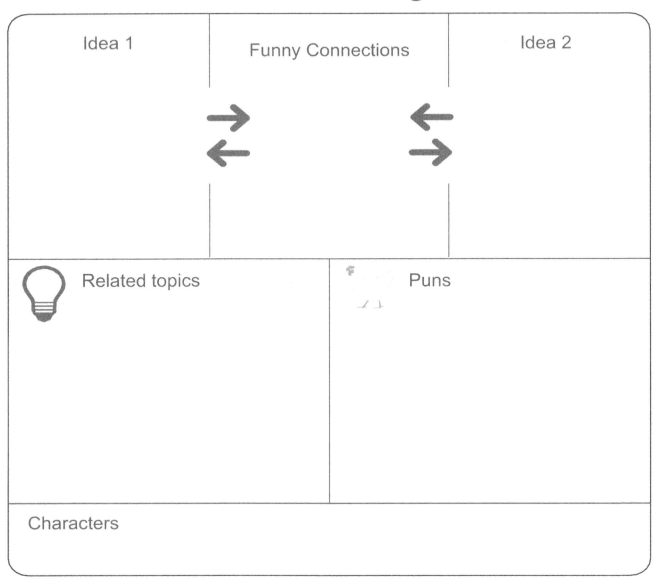

Idea 1	Funny Connections	Idea 2

Related topics

Puns

Characters

Joke

Setup

Punchline

Brainstorming

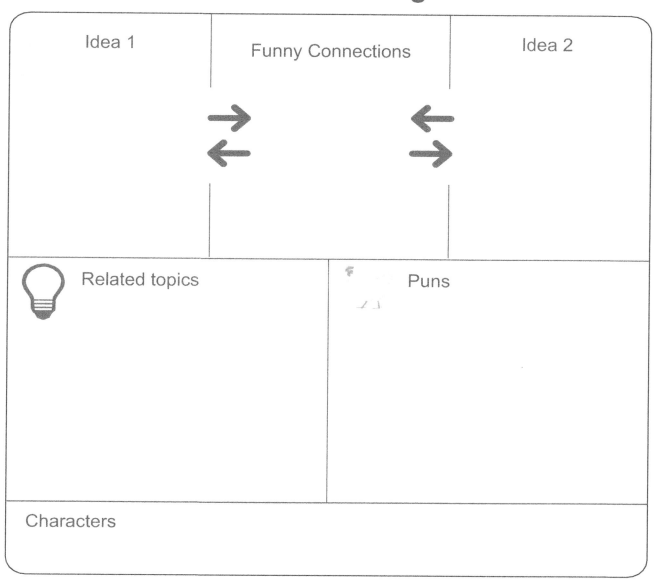

Idea 1	Funny Connections	Idea 2

Related topics

Puns

Characters

Joke

Setup

Punchline

Brainstorming

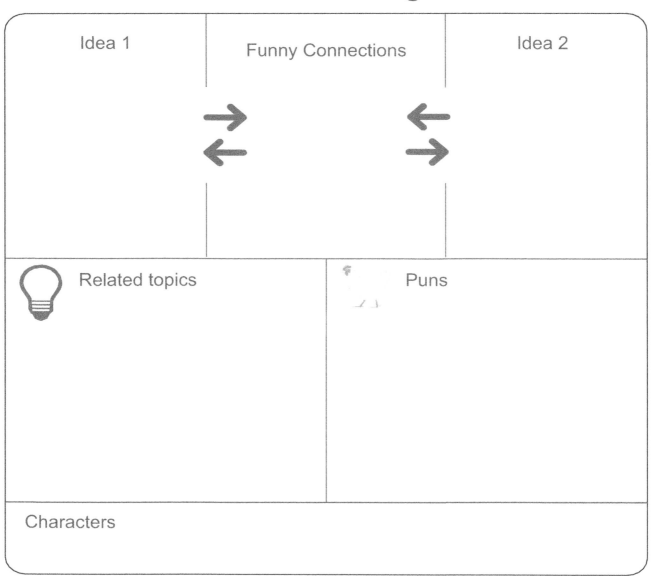

| Idea 1 | Funny Connections | Idea 2 |

Related topics

Puns

Characters

Joke

Setup

Punchline

Brainstorming

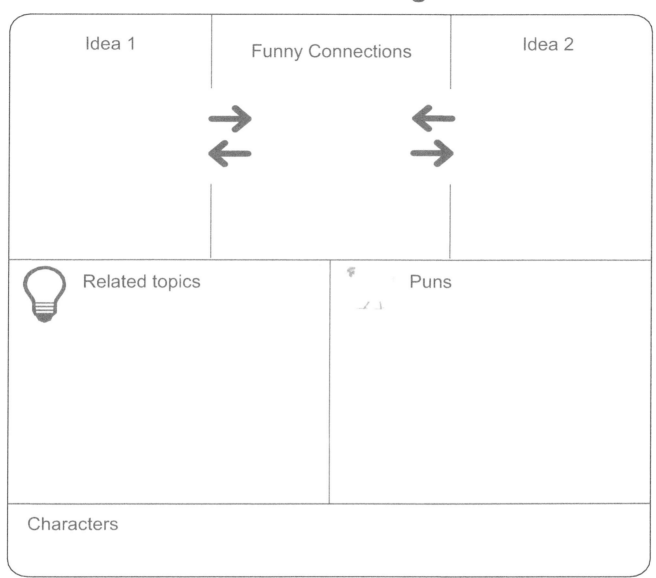

Idea 1	Funny Connections	Idea 2

💡 Related topics

Puns

Characters

Joke

Setup

Punchline

Brainstorming

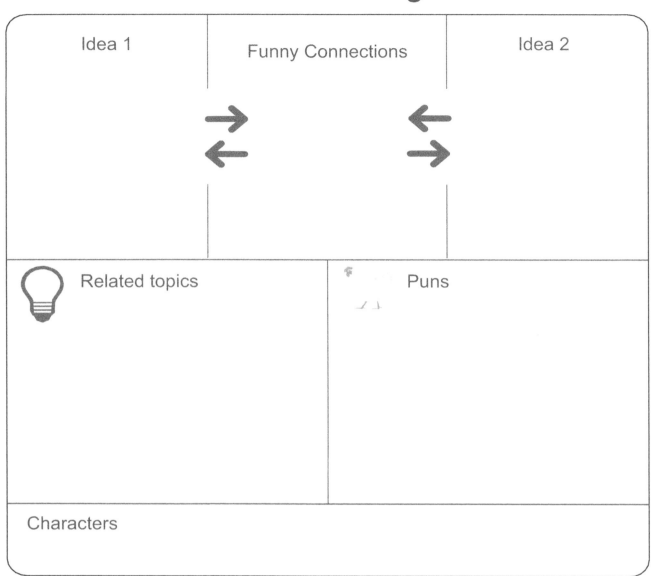

Idea 1	Funny Connections	Idea 2

Related topics

Puns

Characters

Joke

Setup

Punchline

Brainstorming

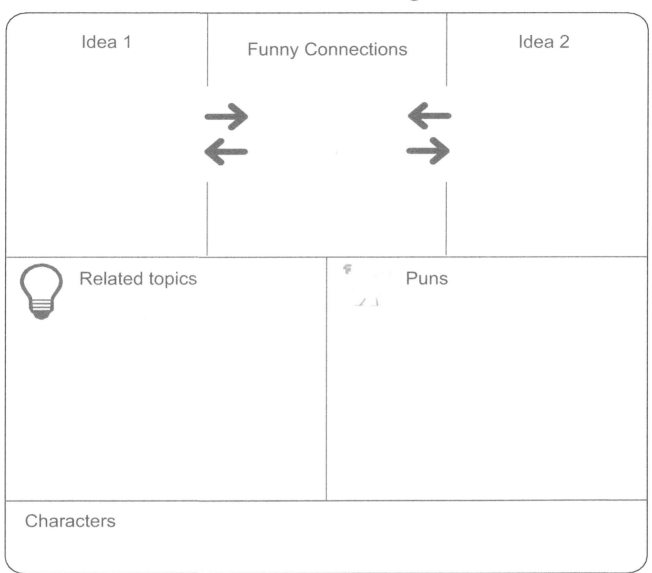

Idea 1	Funny Connections	Idea 2

Related topics

Puns

Characters

Joke

Setup

Punchline

Brainstorming

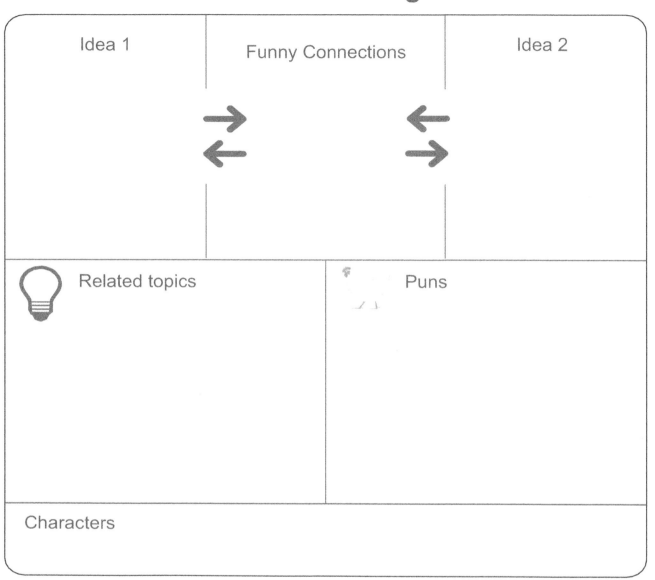

Idea 1	Funny Connections	Idea 2

Related topics

Puns

Characters

Joke

Setup

Punchline

Brainstorming

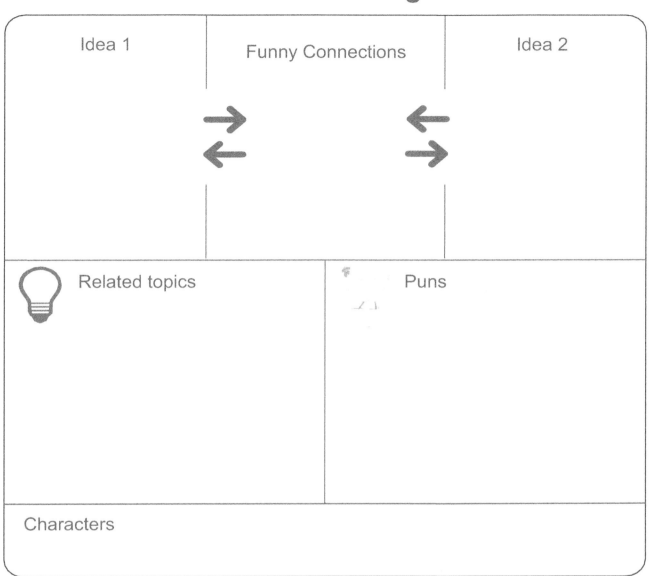

Idea 1	Funny Connections	Idea 2

Related topics

Puns

Characters

Joke

Setup

Punchline

Brainstorming

Idea 1	Funny Connections	Idea 2

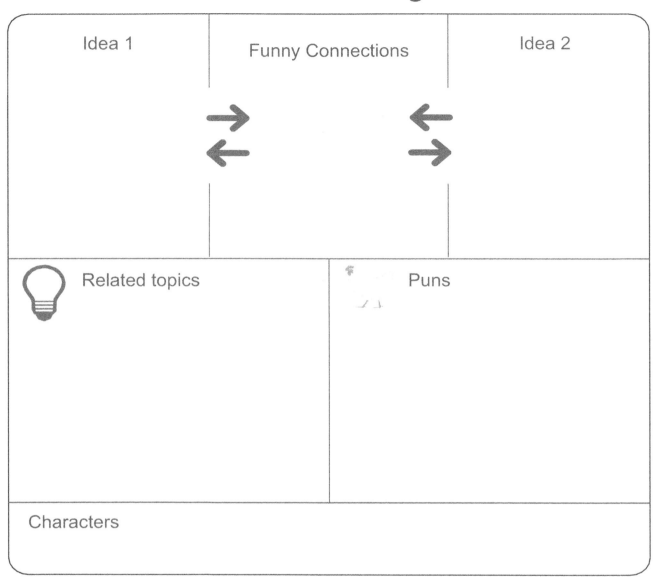

Related topics

Puns

Characters

Joke

Setup

Punchline

Brainstorming

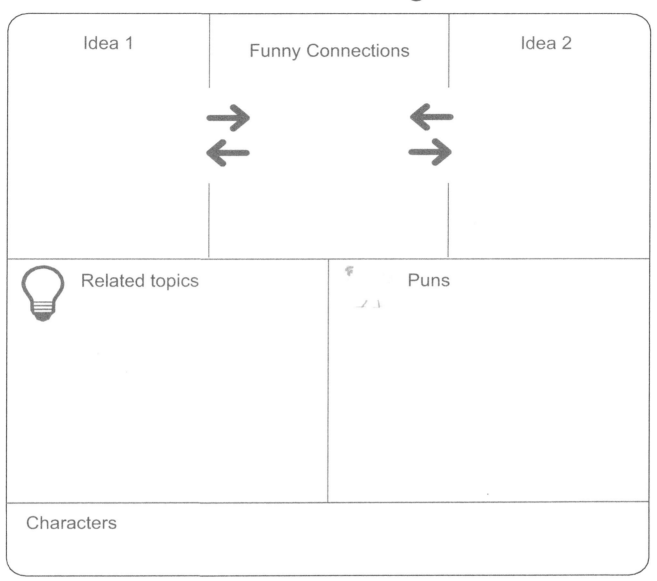

| Idea 1 | Funny Connections | Idea 2 |

Related topics

Puns

Characters

Joke

Setup

Punchline

Brainstorming

Idea 1	Funny Connections	Idea 2

Related topics	Puns

Characters

Joke

Setup

Punchline

Brainstorming

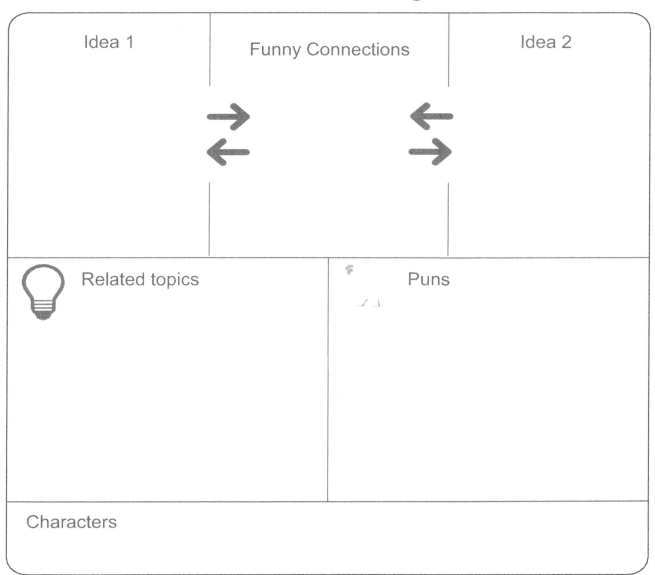

| Idea 1 | Funny Connections | Idea 2 |

Related topics

Puns

Characters

Joke

Setup

Punchline

Brainstorming

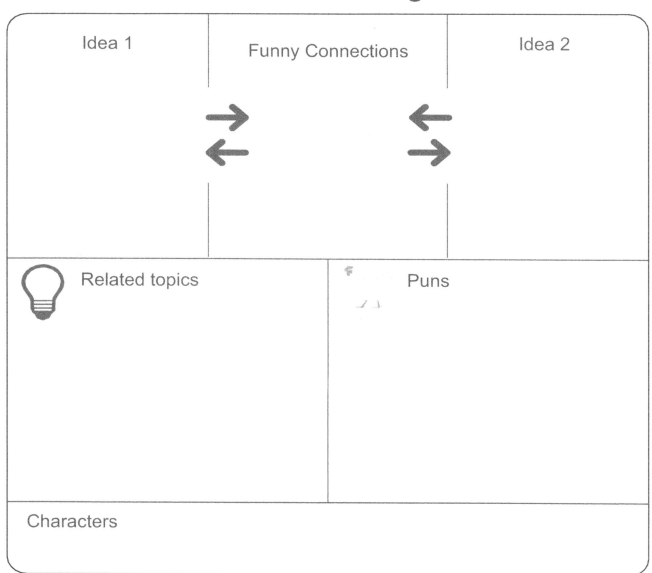

Idea 1	Funny Connections	Idea 2

Related topics

Puns

Characters

Joke

Setup

Punchline

Brainstorming

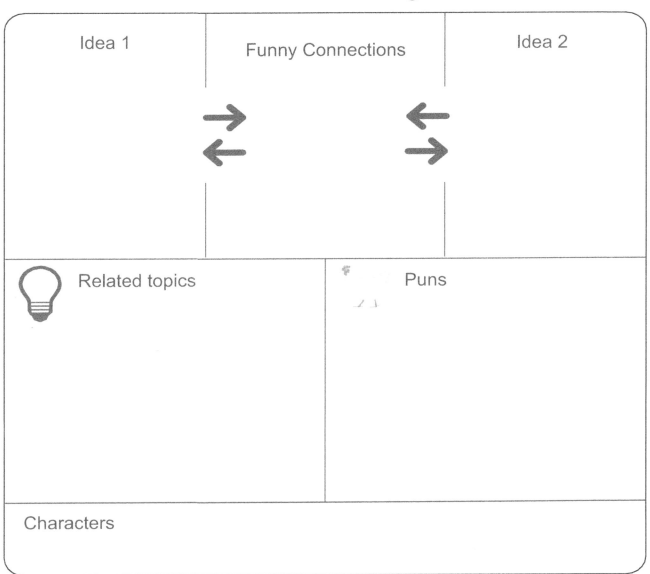

Idea 1	Funny Connections	Idea 2

Related topics

Puns

Characters

Joke

Setup

Punchline

Brainstorming

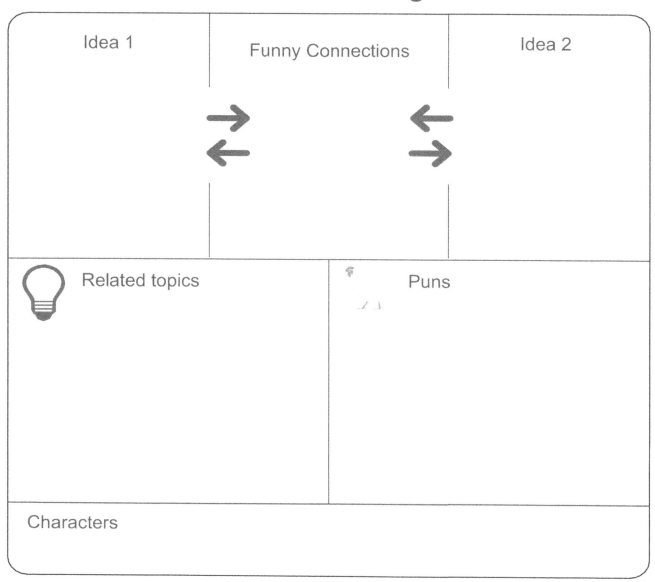

Idea 1	Funny Connections	Idea 2

Related topics

Puns

Characters

Joke

Setup

Punchline

Brainstorming

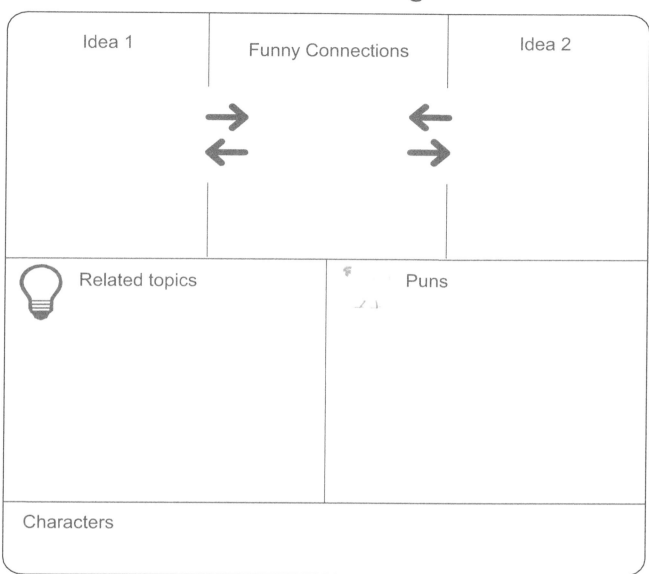

| Idea 1 | Funny Connections | Idea 2 |

Related topics

Puns

Characters

Joke

Setup

Punchline

Brainstorming

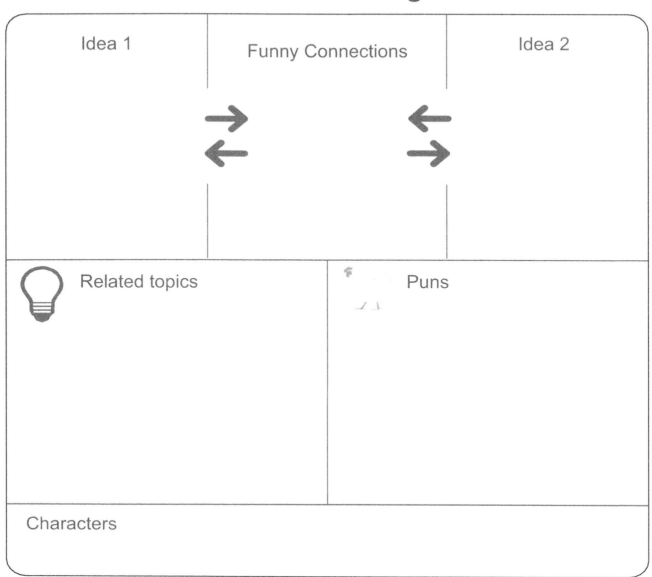

Idea 1	Funny Connections	Idea 2

Related topics

Puns

Characters

Joke

Setup

Punchline

Brainstorming

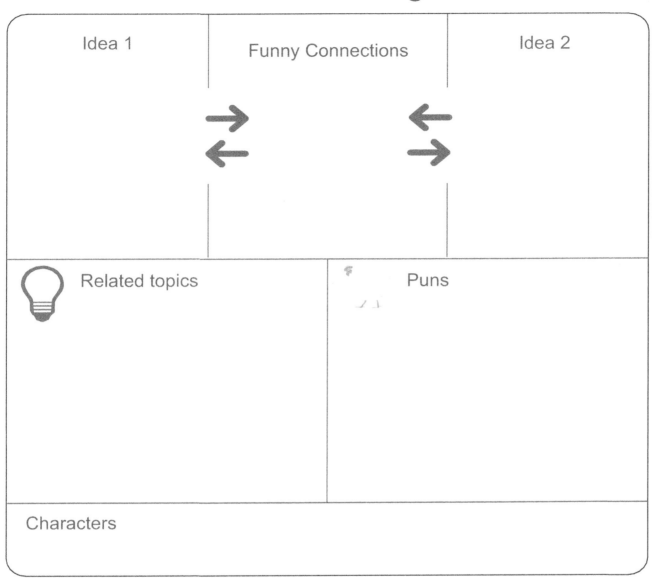

Idea 1	Funny Connections	Idea 2

💡 Related topics

Puns

Characters

Joke

Setup

Punchline

Brainstorming

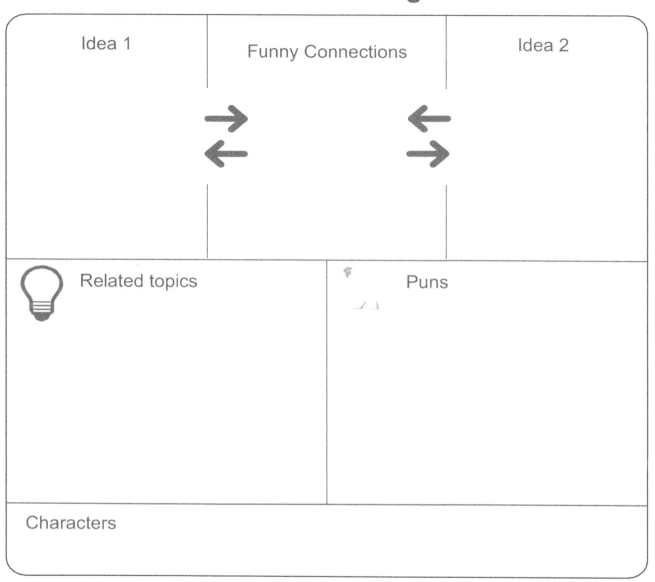

Idea 1	Funny Connections	Idea 2

Related topics

Puns

Characters

Joke

Setup

Punchline

Brainstorming

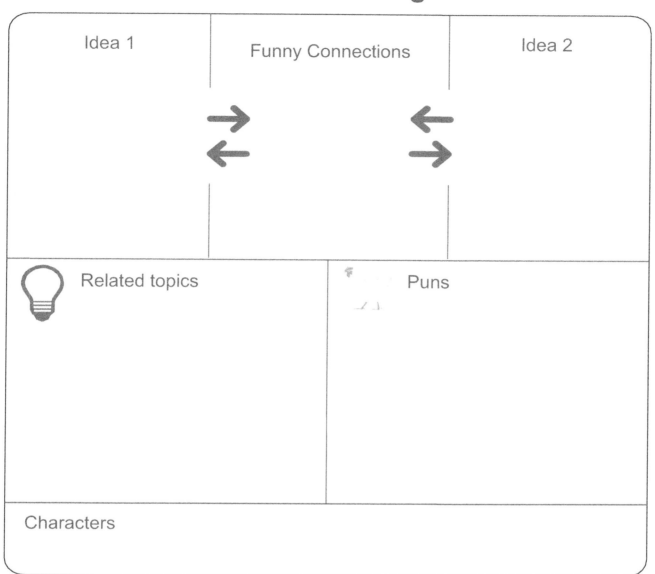

Idea 1	Funny Connections	Idea 2

Related topics

Puns

Characters

Joke

Setup

Punchline

Brainstorming

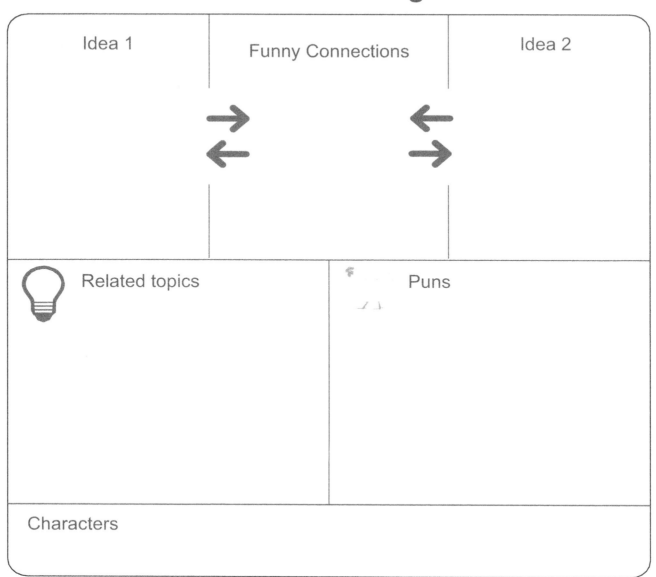

Idea 1	Funny Connections	Idea 2

Related topics

Puns

Characters

Joke

Setup

Punchline

Brainstorming

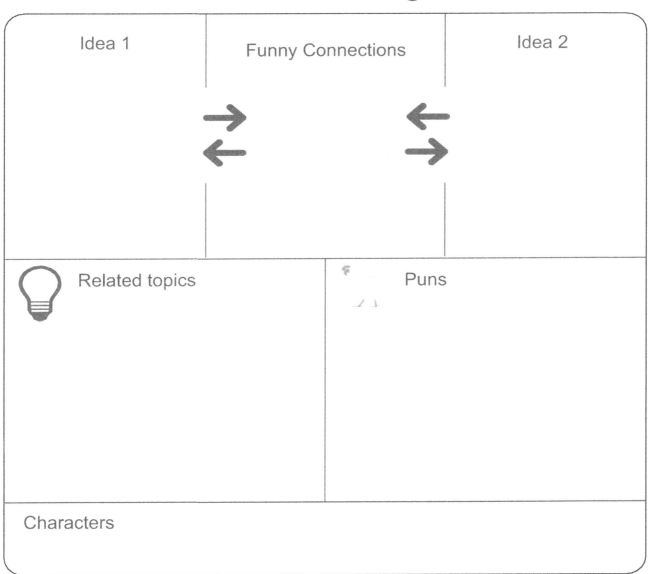

Idea 1	Funny Connections	Idea 2

Related topics

Puns

Characters

Joke

Setup

Punchline

Brainstorming

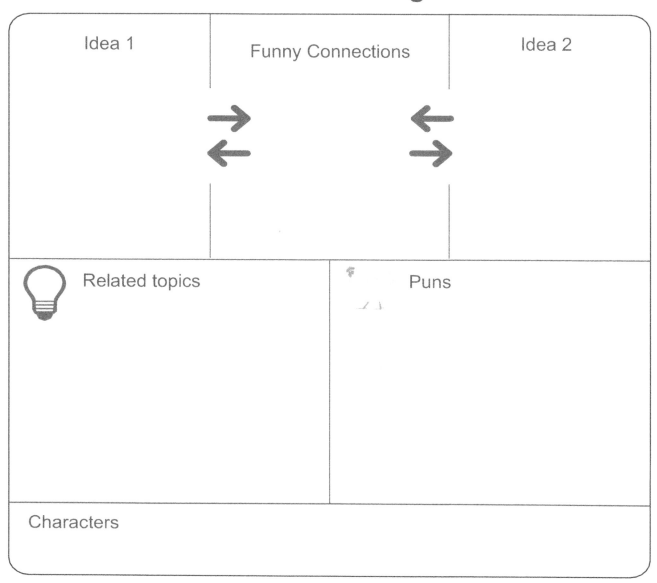

Idea 1	Funny Connections	Idea 2

Related topics

Puns

Characters

Joke

Setup

Punchline

Brainstorming

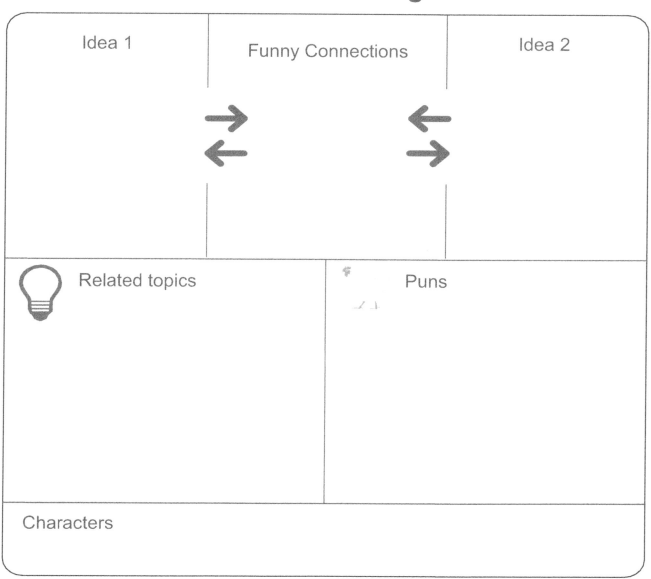

Idea 1	Funny Connections	Idea 2

Related topics

Puns

Characters

Joke

Setup

Punchline

Brainstorming

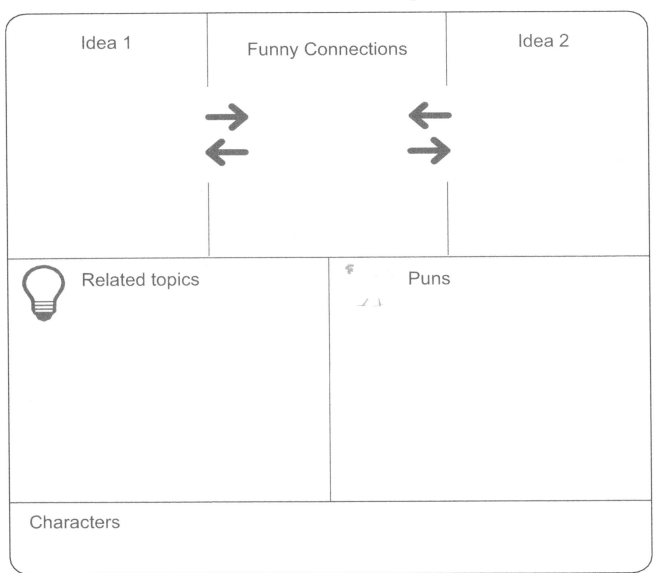

Idea 1	Funny Connections	Idea 2

Related topics

Puns

Characters

Joke

Setup

Punchline

Brainstorming

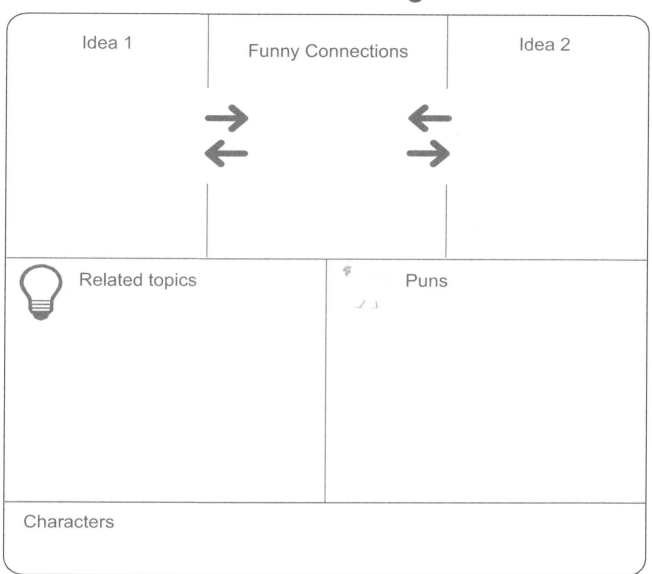

Idea 1	Funny Connections	Idea 2

Related topics

Puns

Characters

Joke

Setup

Punchline

Brainstorming

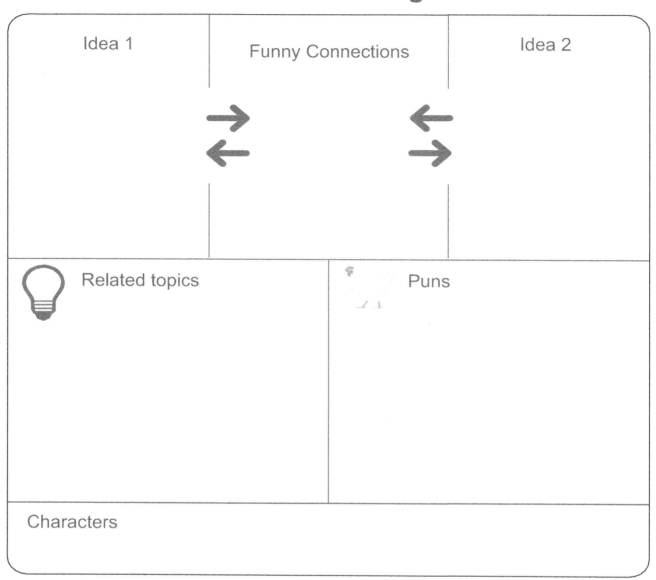

Idea 1	Funny Connections	Idea 2

Related topics

Puns

Characters

Joke

Setup

Punchline

Brainstorming

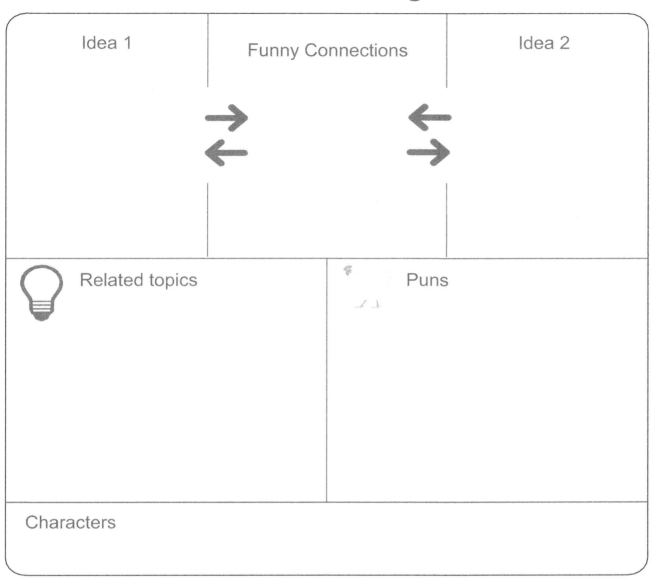

Idea 1	Funny Connections	Idea 2

Related topics

Puns

Characters

Joke

Setup

Punchline

Brainstorming

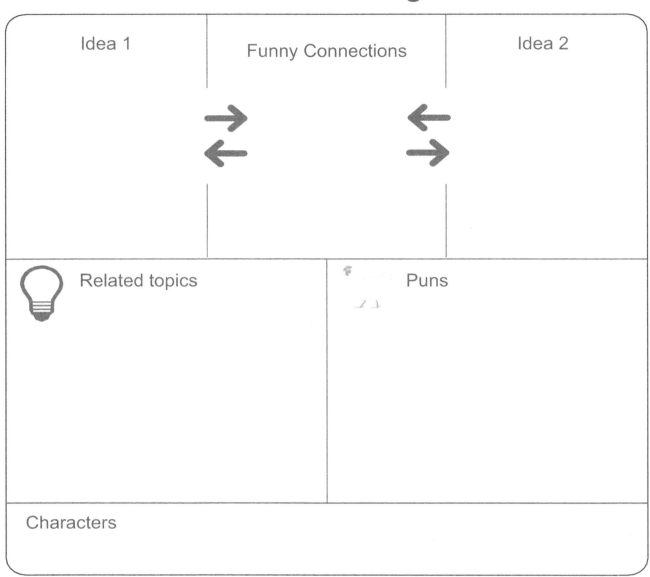

Idea 1	Funny Connections	Idea 2

Related topics

Puns

Characters

Joke

Setup

Punchline

Brainstorming

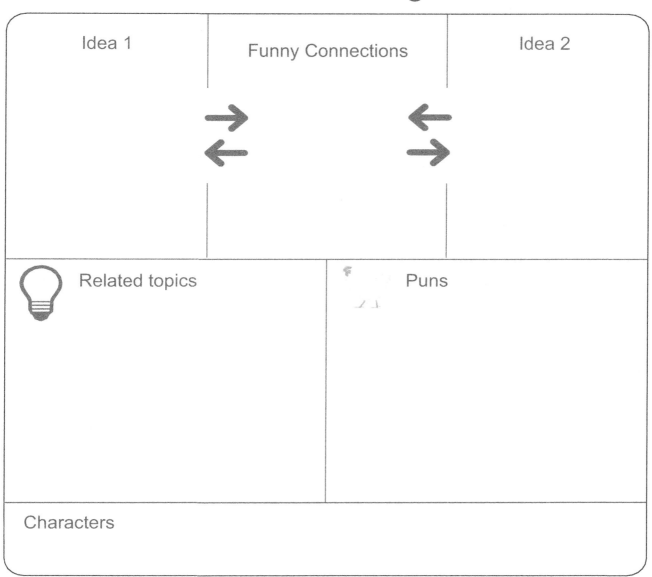

Idea 1	Funny Connections	Idea 2

Related topics

Puns

Characters

Joke

Setup

Punchline

Brainstorming

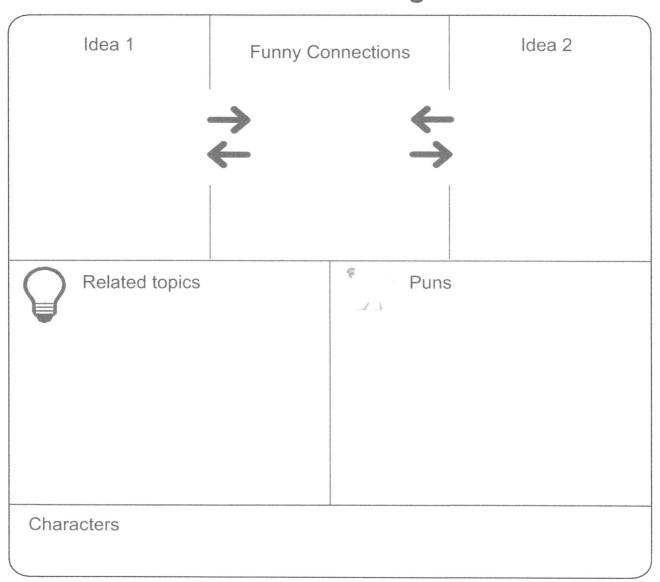

Idea 1	Funny Connections	Idea 2

Related topics

Puns

Characters

Joke

Setup

Punchline

Brainstorming

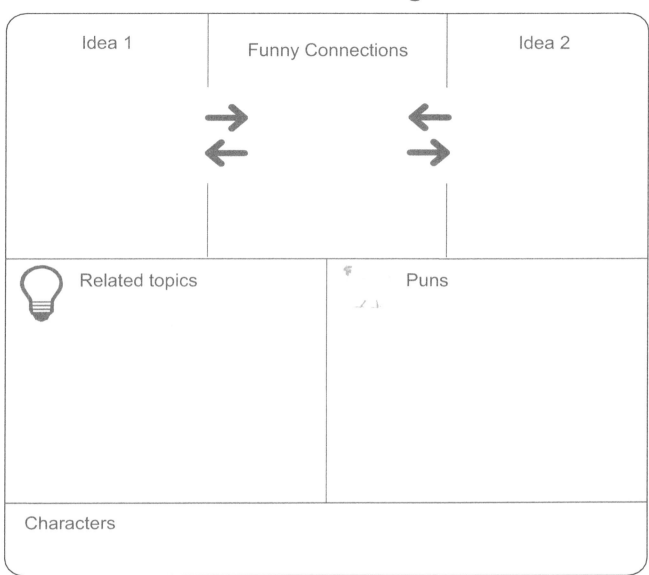

Idea 1	Funny Connections	Idea 2

Related topics

Puns

Characters

Joke

Setup

Punchline

Brainstorming

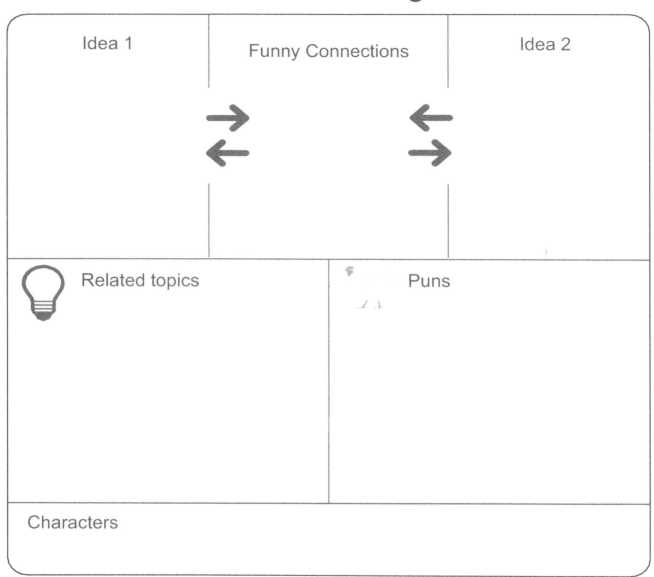

Idea 1	Funny Connections	Idea 2

Related topics

Puns

Characters

Joke

Setup

Punchline

Brainstorming

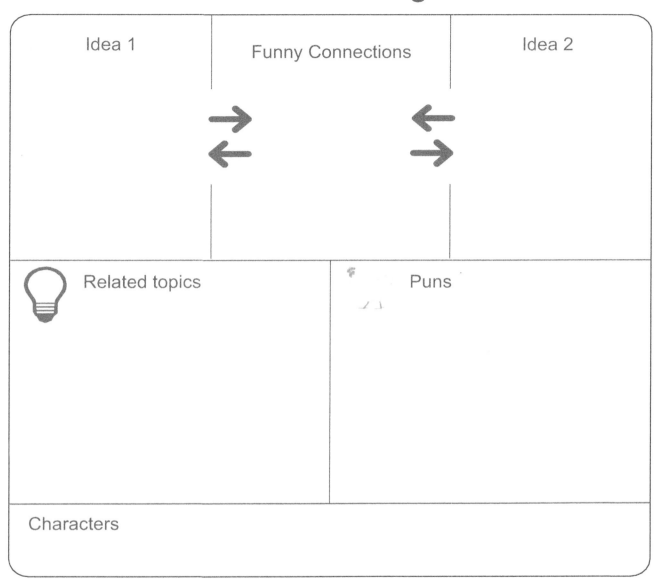

Idea 1	Funny Connections	Idea 2

Related topics

Puns

Characters

Joke

Setup

Punchline

Brainstorming

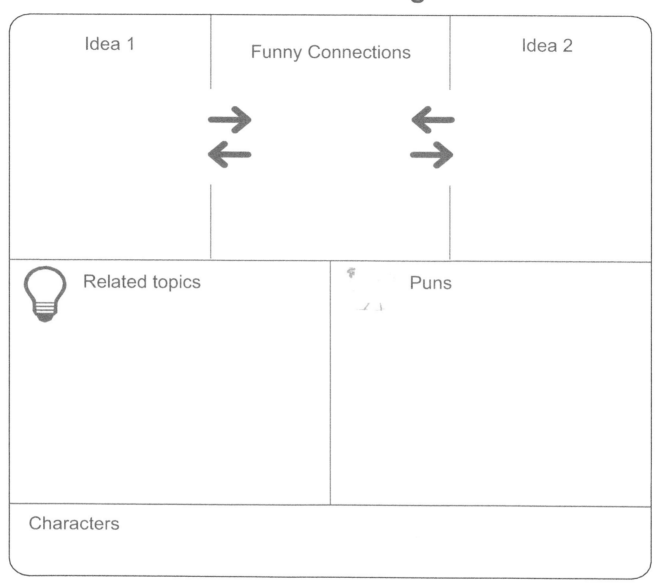

Idea 1	Funny Connections	Idea 2

Related topics

Puns

Characters

Joke

Setup

Punchline

Brainstorming

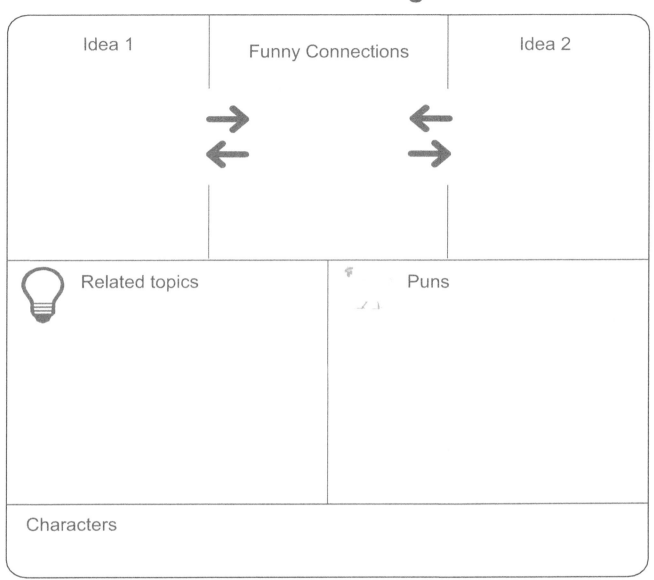

Idea 1	Funny Connections	Idea 2

Related topics

Puns

Characters

Joke

Setup

Punchline

Brainstorming

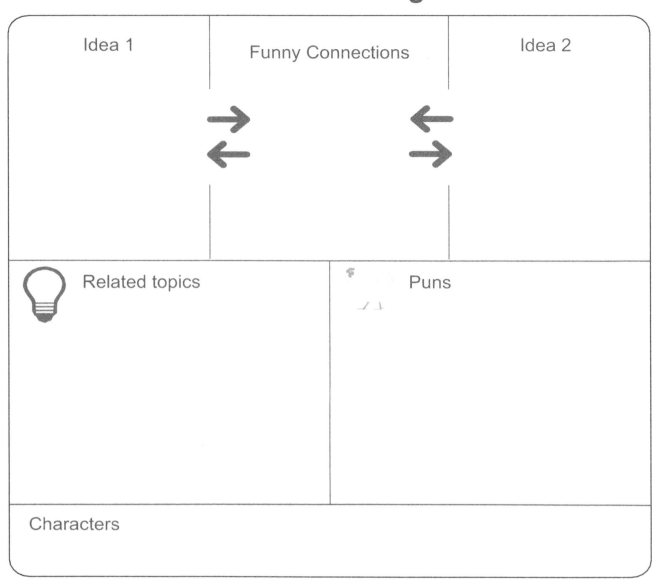

| Idea 1 | Funny Connections | Idea 2 |

Related topics

Puns

Characters

Joke

Setup

Punchline

Brainstorming

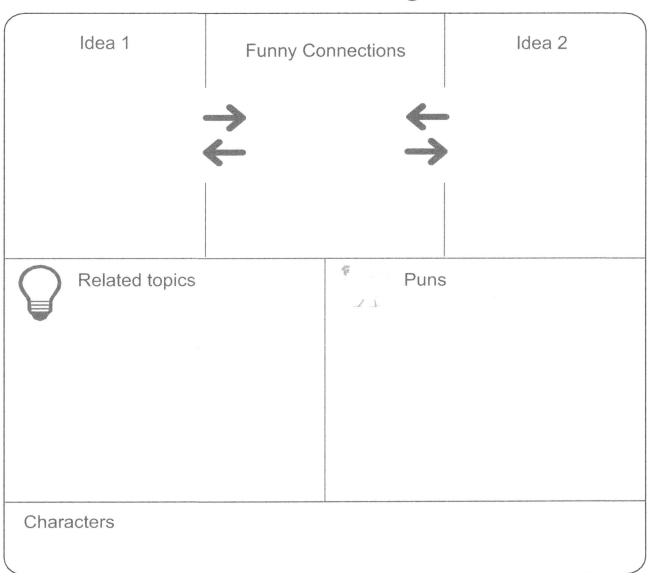

Idea 1	Funny Connections	Idea 2

Related topics

Puns

Characters

Joke

Setup

Punchline

Brainstorming

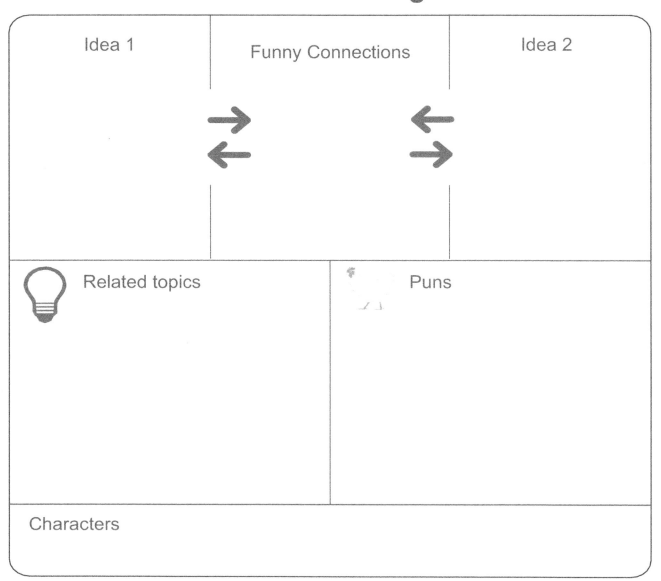

| Idea 1 | Funny Connections | Idea 2 |

Related topics

Puns

Characters

Joke

Setup

Punchline

Brainstorming

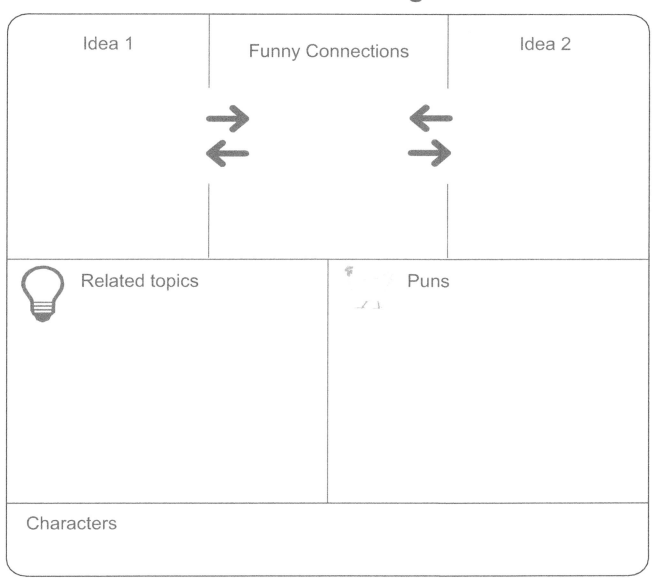

Idea 1	Funny Connections	Idea 2

Related topics

Puns

Characters

Joke

Setup

Punchline

Brainstorming

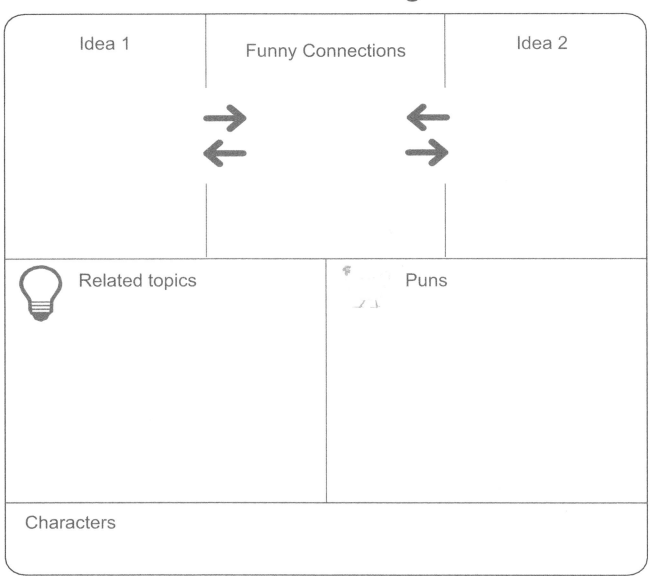

| Idea 1 | Funny Connections | Idea 2 |

Related topics

Puns

Characters

Joke

Setup

Punchline

Brainstorming

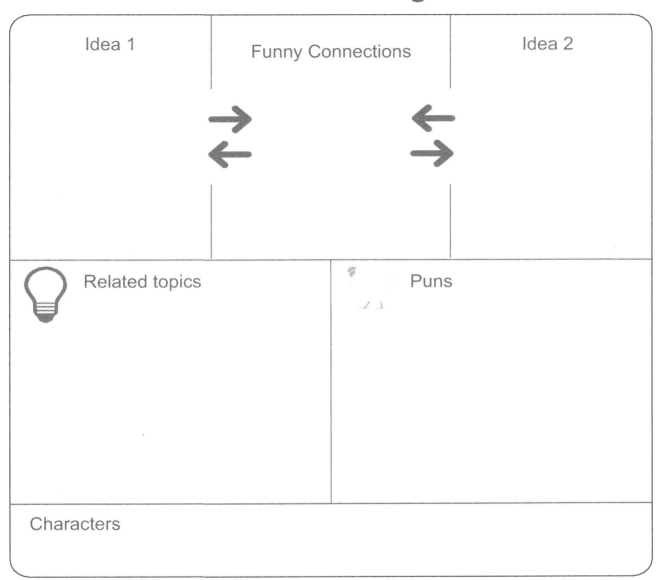

Idea 1	Funny Connections	Idea 2

Related topics

Puns

Characters

Joke

Setup

Punchline

Brainstorming

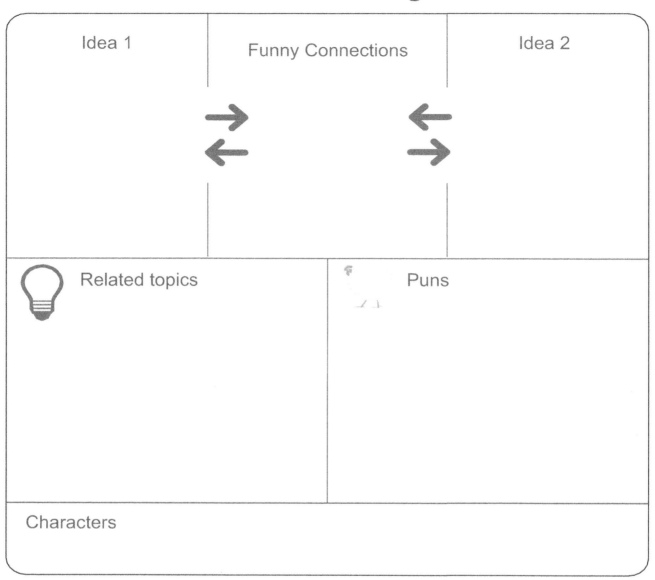

Idea 1	Funny Connections	Idea 2

Related topics

Puns

Characters

Joke

Setup

Punchline

Brainstorming

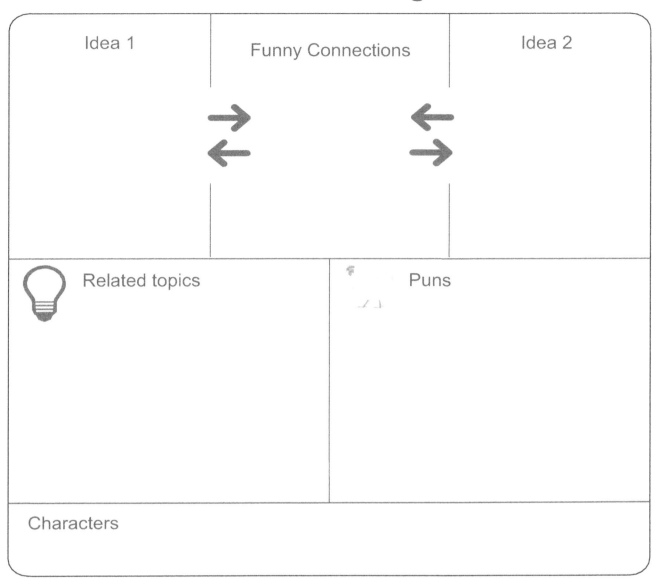

Idea 1	Funny Connections	Idea 2

Related topics

Puns

Characters

Joke

Setup

Punchline

Brainstorming

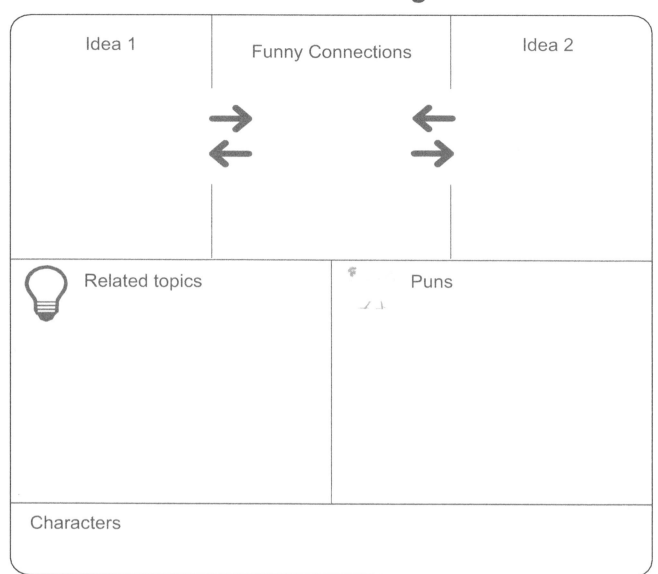

| Idea 1 | Funny Connections | Idea 2 |

Related topics

Puns

Characters

Joke

Setup

Punchline

Brainstorming

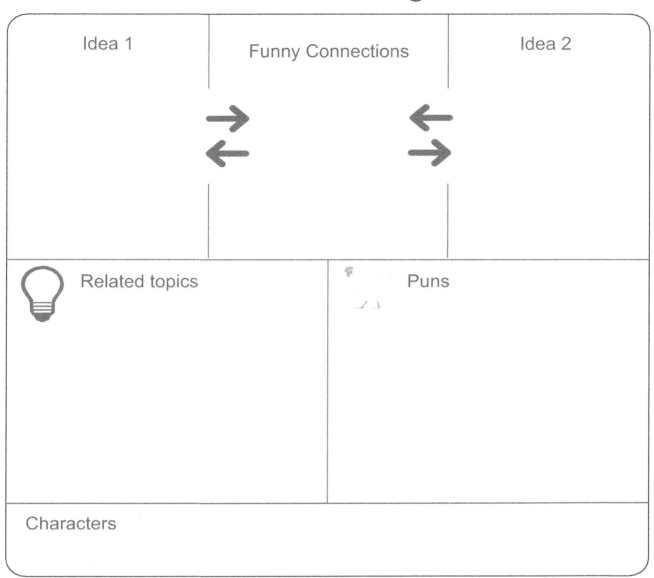

Idea 1	Funny Connections	Idea 2

Related topics

Puns

Characters

Joke

Setup

Punchline

Brainstorming

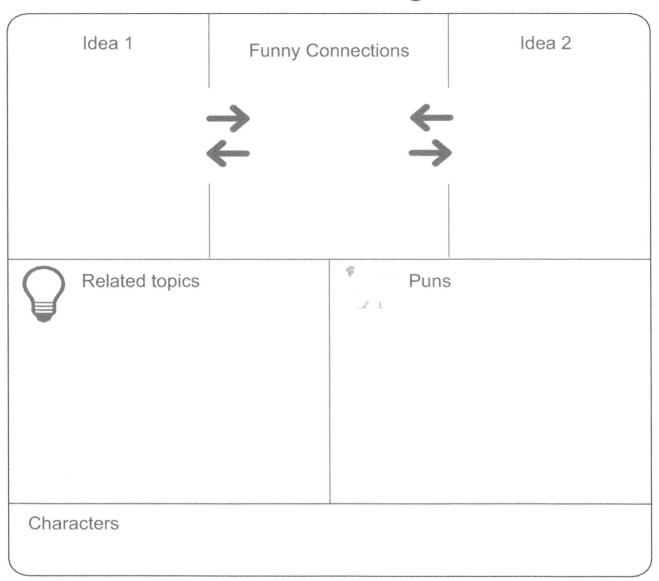

Idea 1	Funny Connections	Idea 2

Related topics

Puns

Characters

Joke

Setup

Punchline

Brainstorming

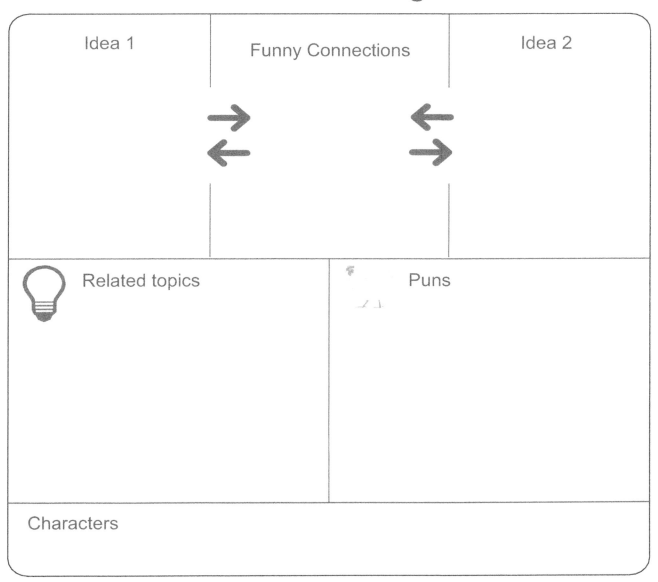

Idea 1	Funny Connections	Idea 2

Related topics

Puns

Characters

Joke

Setup

Punchline

Brainstorming

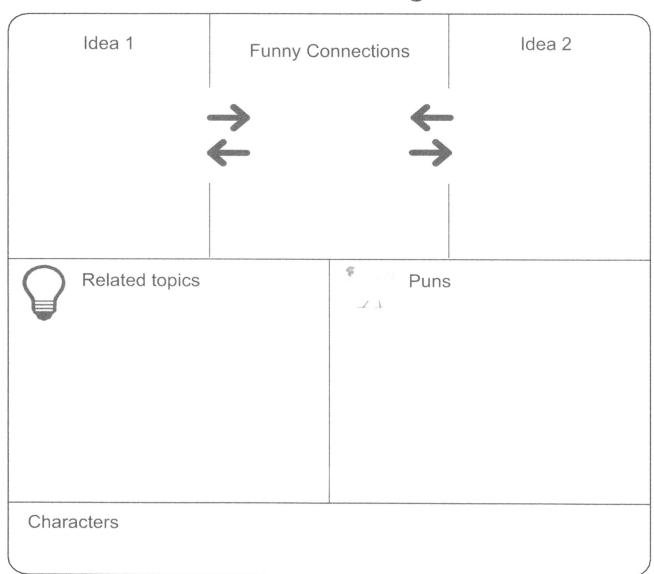

Idea 1	Funny Connections	Idea 2

Related topics

Puns

Characters

Joke

Setup

Punchline

Brainstorming

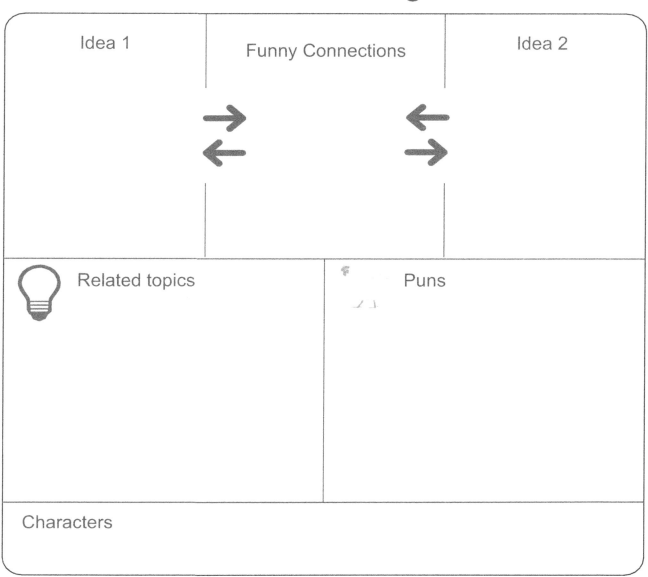

Idea 1	Funny Connections	Idea 2

Related topics

Puns

Characters

Joke

Setup

Punchline

Brainstorming

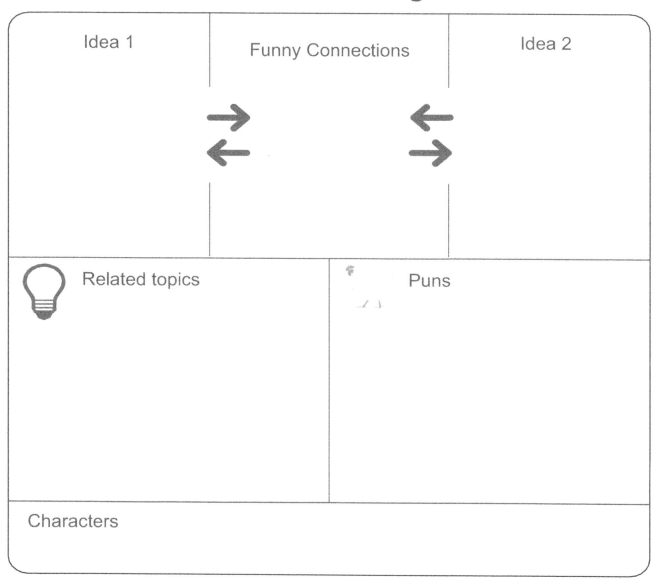

Idea 1	Funny Connections	Idea 2

Related topics

Puns

Characters

Joke

Setup

Punchline

Brainstorming

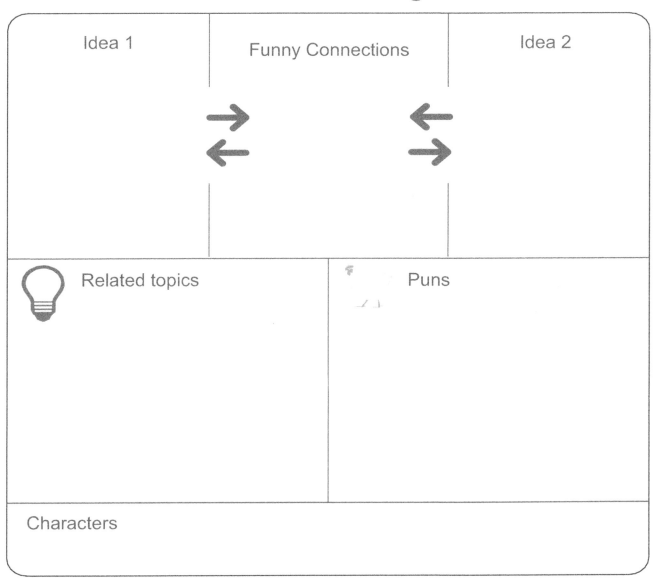

Idea 1	Funny Connections	Idea 2

Related topics

Puns

Characters

Joke

Setup

Punchline

Brainstorming

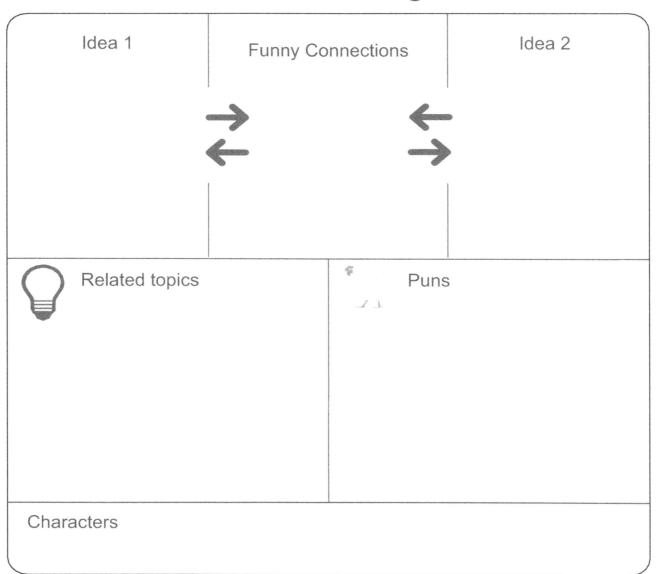

Idea 1	Funny Connections	Idea 2

Related topics

Puns

Characters

Joke

Setup

Punchline

Brainstorming

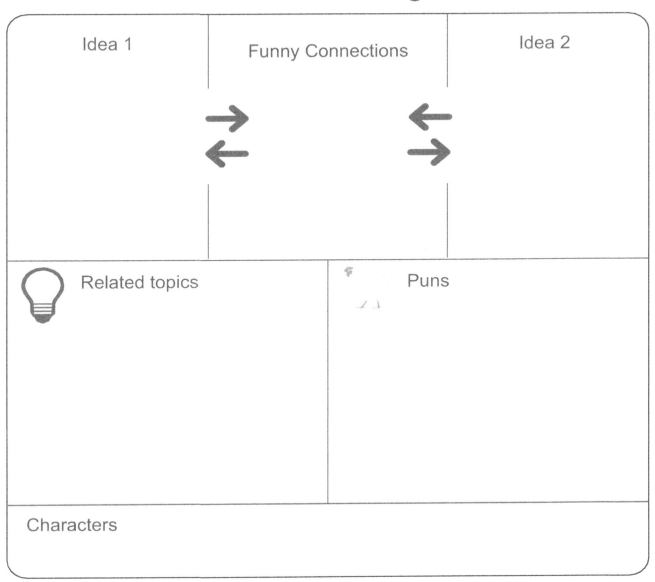

Idea 1	Funny Connections	Idea 2

Related topics

Puns

Characters

Joke

Setup

Punchline

Brainstorming

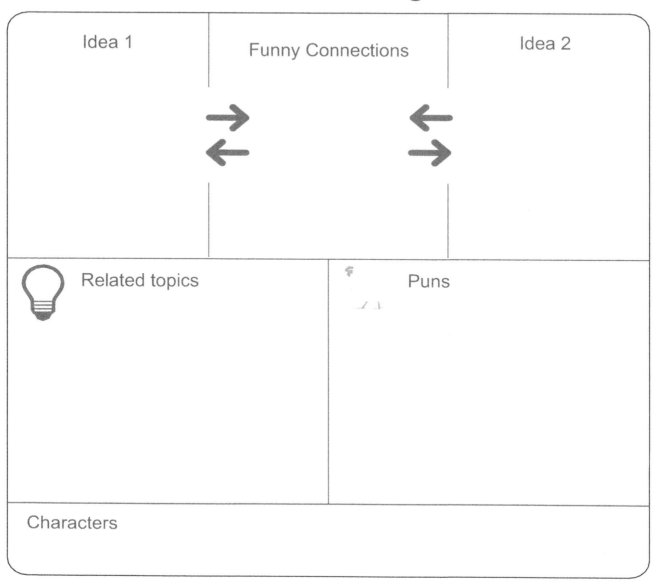

Idea 1	Funny Connections	Idea 2

Related topics

Puns

Characters

Joke

Setup

Punchline

Brainstorming

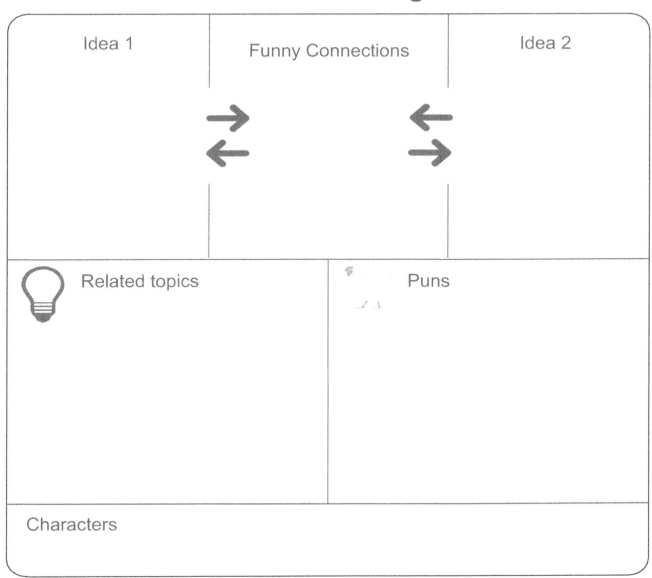

Idea 1	Funny Connections	Idea 2

Related topics

Puns

Characters

Joke

Setup

Punchline

Brainstorming

Idea 1	Funny Connections	Idea 2

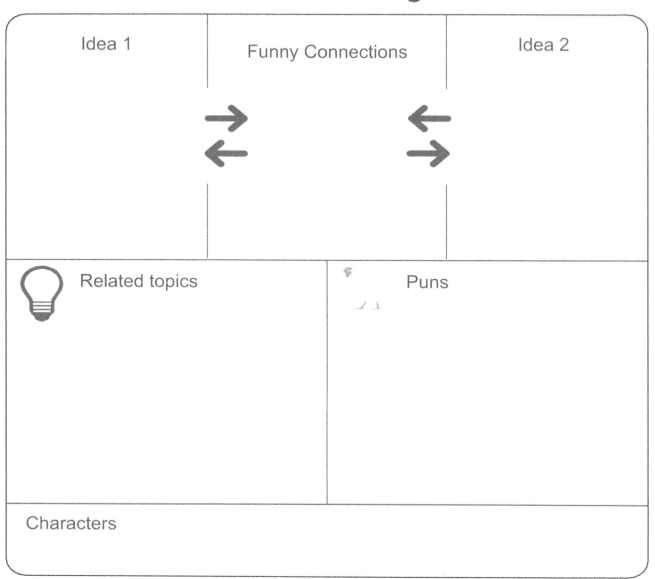

Related topics

Puns

Characters

Joke

Setup

Punchline

Brainstorming

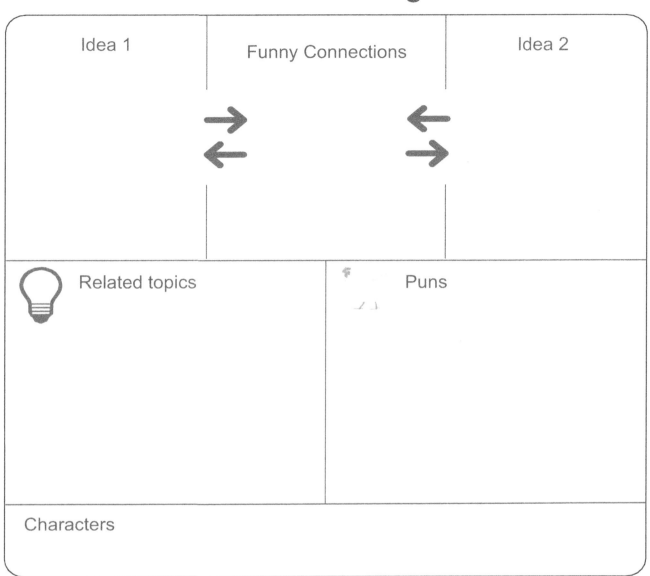

Idea 1	Funny Connections	Idea 2

Related topics

Puns

Characters

Joke

Setup

Punchline

Brainstorming

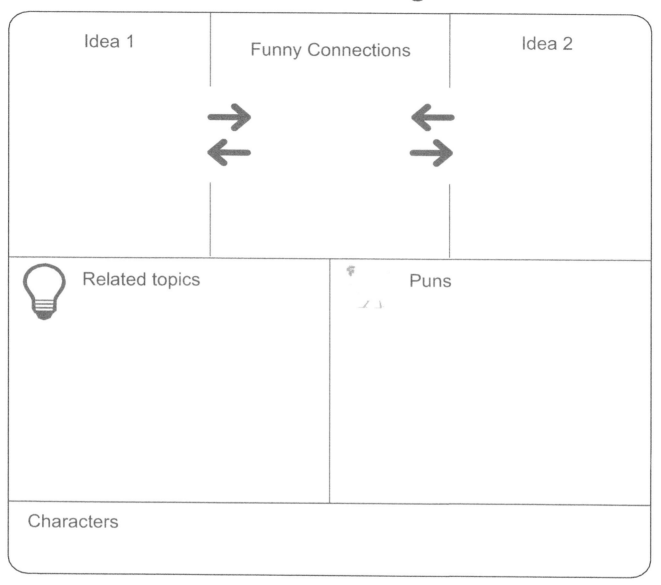

Idea 1	Funny Connections	Idea 2

Related topics

Puns

Characters

Joke

Setup

Punchline

Brainstorming

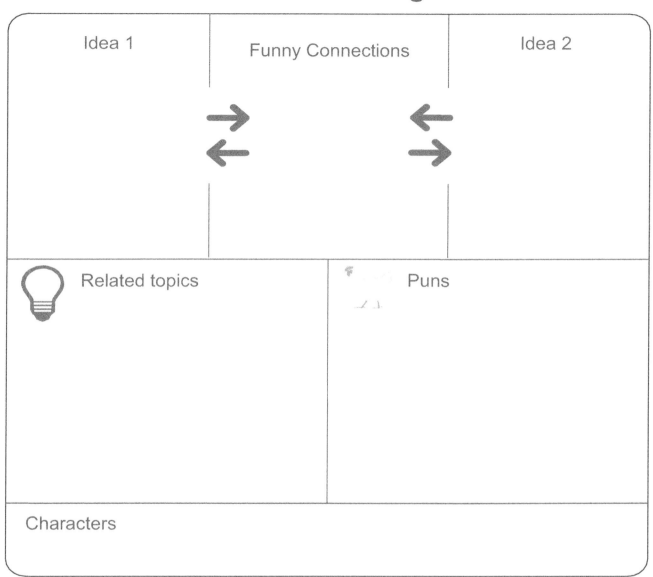

Idea 1	Funny Connections	Idea 2

Related topics

Puns

Characters

Joke

Setup

Punchline

Brainstorming

Idea 1	Funny Connections	Idea 2

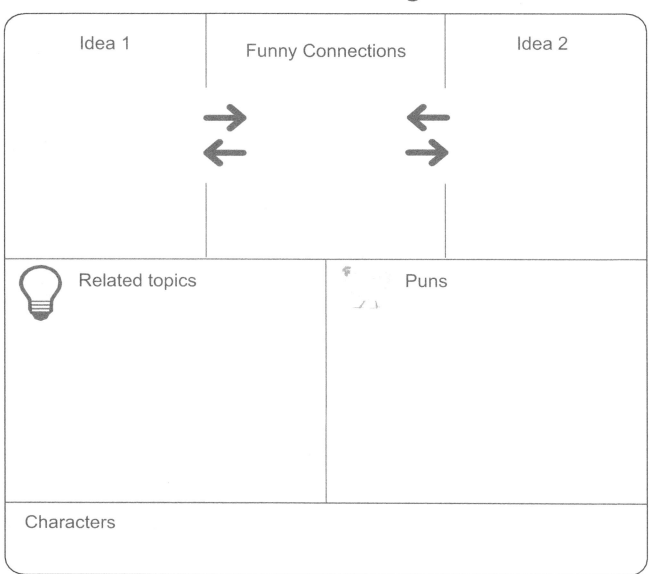

Related topics

Puns

Characters

Joke

Setup

Punchline

Brainstorming

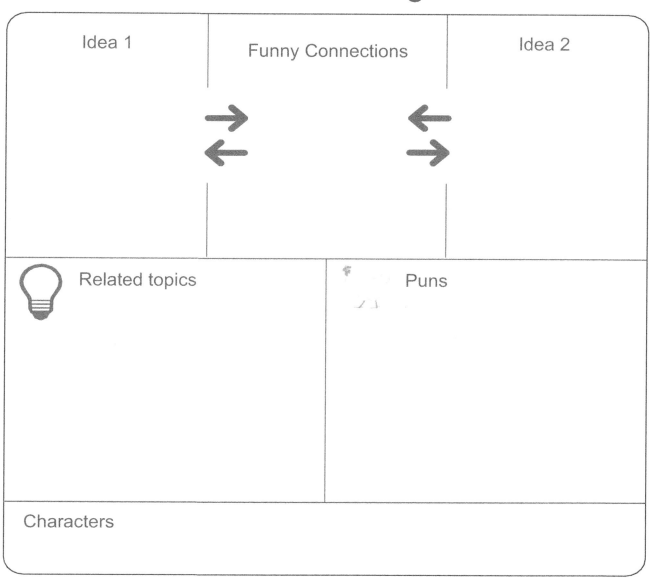

Idea 1	Funny Connections	Idea 2

Related topics

Puns

Characters

Joke

Setup

Punchline

Brainstorming

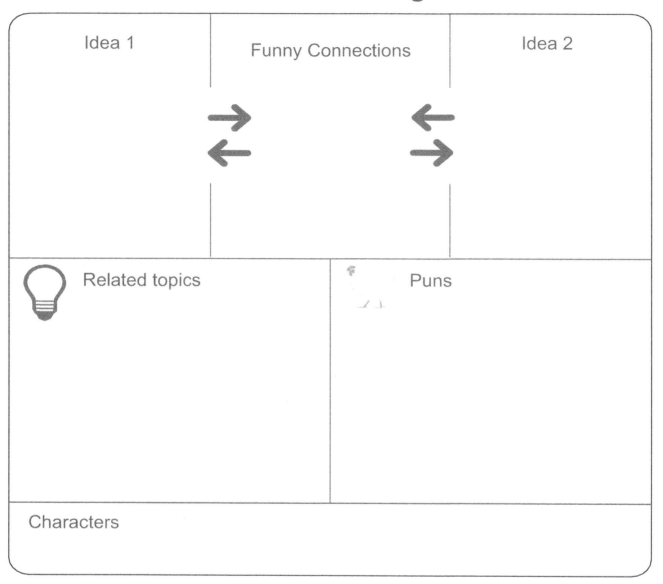

Idea 1	Funny Connections	Idea 2

Related topics

Puns

Characters

Joke

Setup

Punchline

Brainstorming

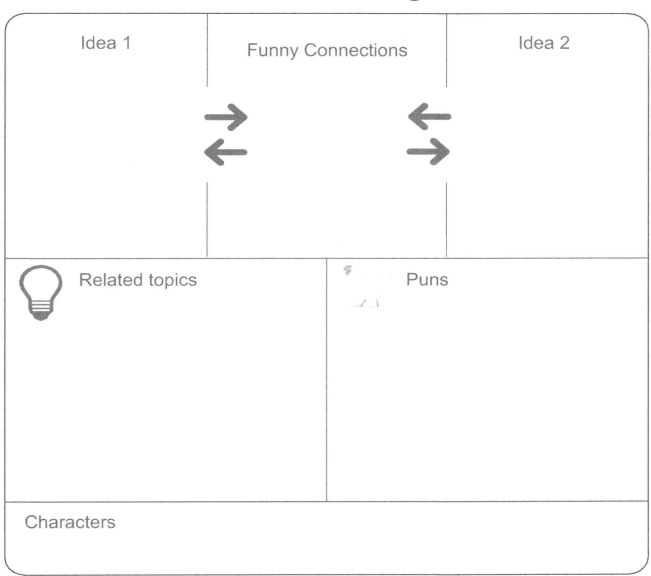

| Idea 1 | Funny Connections | Idea 2 |

💡 Related topics

Puns

Characters

Joke

Setup

Punchline

Brainstorming

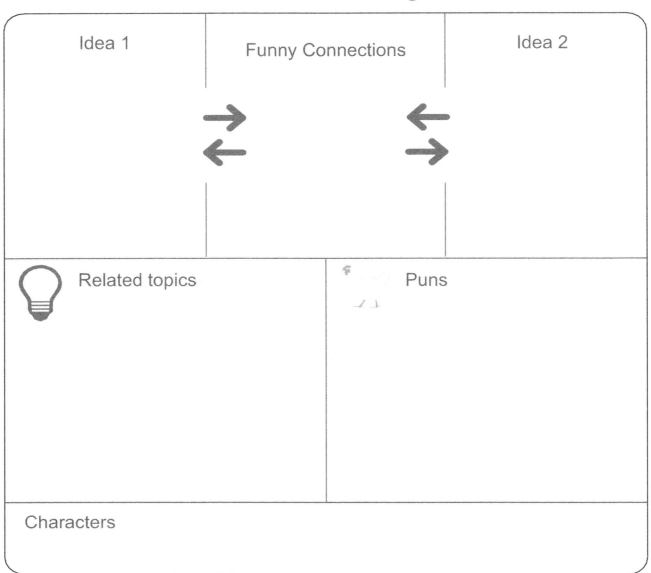

Idea 1	Funny Connections	Idea 2

Related topics

Puns

Characters

Joke

Setup

Punchline

Brainstorming

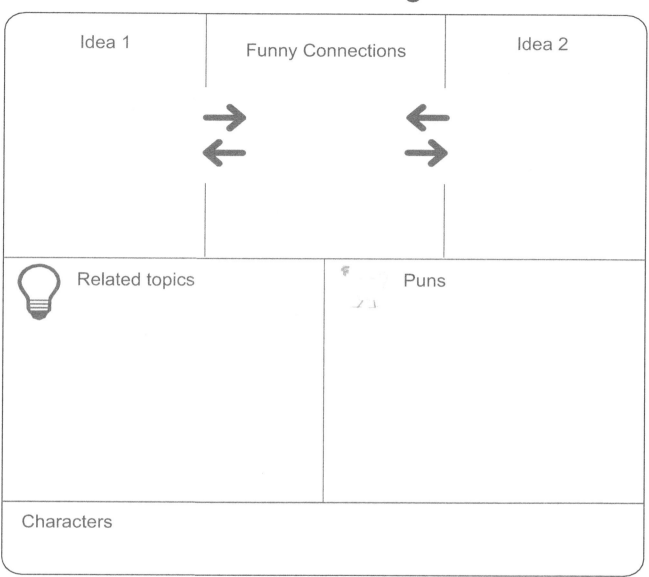

Idea 1	Funny Connections	Idea 2

Related topics

Puns

Characters

Joke

Setup

Punchline

Brainstorming

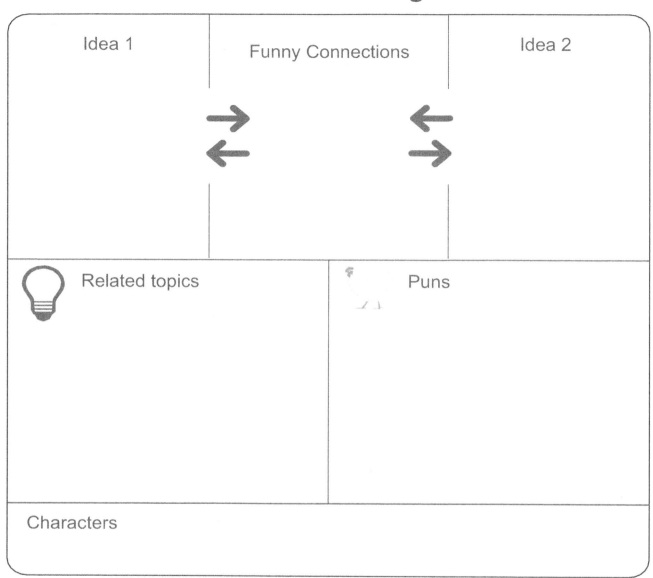

Idea 1	Funny Connections	Idea 2

Related topics

Puns

Characters

Joke

Setup

Punchline

Brainstorming

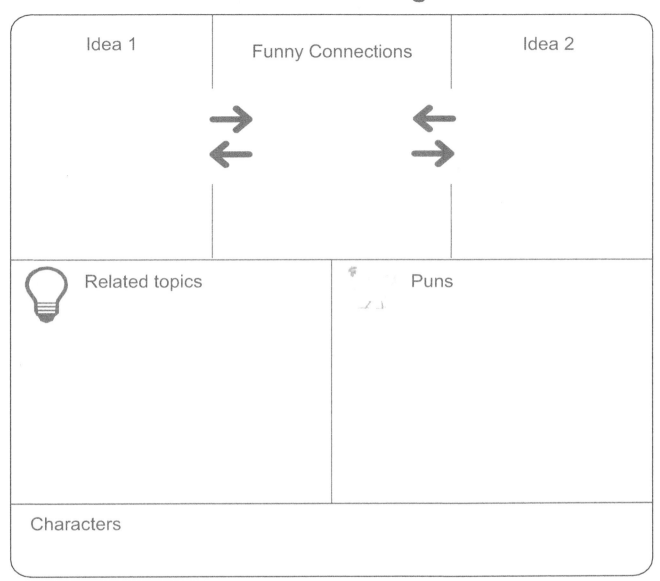

Idea 1	Funny Connections	Idea 2

Related topics

Puns

Characters

Joke

Setup

Punchline

Brainstorming

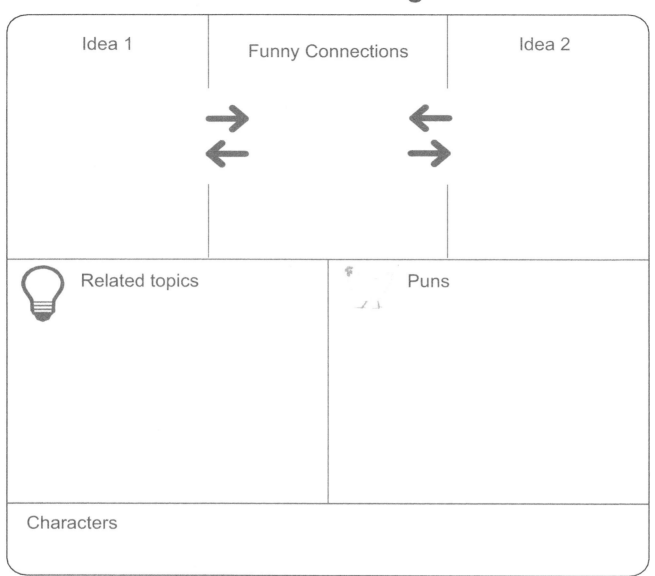

Idea 1	Funny Connections	Idea 2

Related topics

Puns

Characters

Joke

Setup

Punchline

Brainstorming

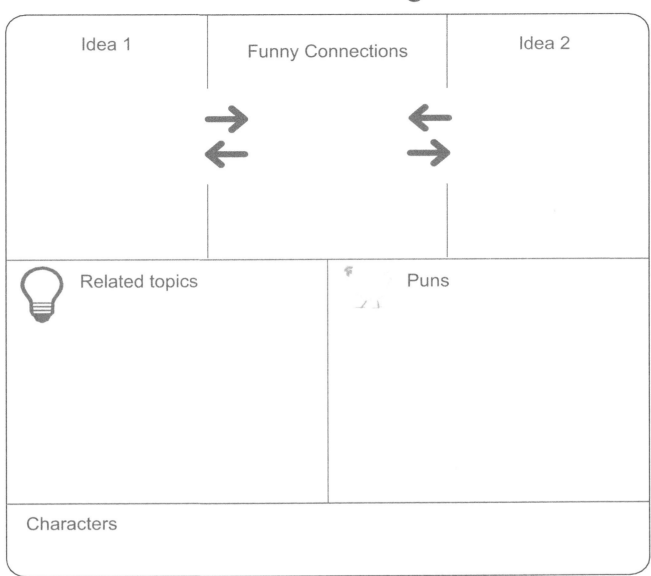

Idea 1	Funny Connections	Idea 2

Related topics

Puns

Characters

Joke

Setup

Punchline

Brainstorming

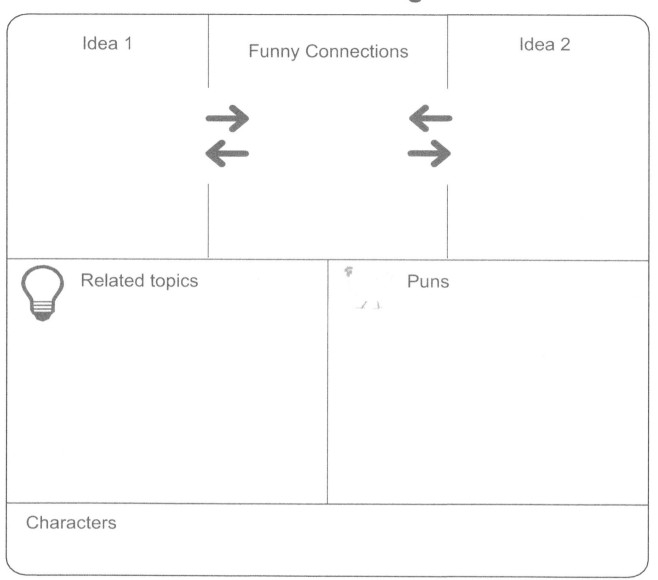

Idea 1	Funny Connections	Idea 2

Related topics

Puns

Characters

Joke

Setup

Punchline

Brainstorming

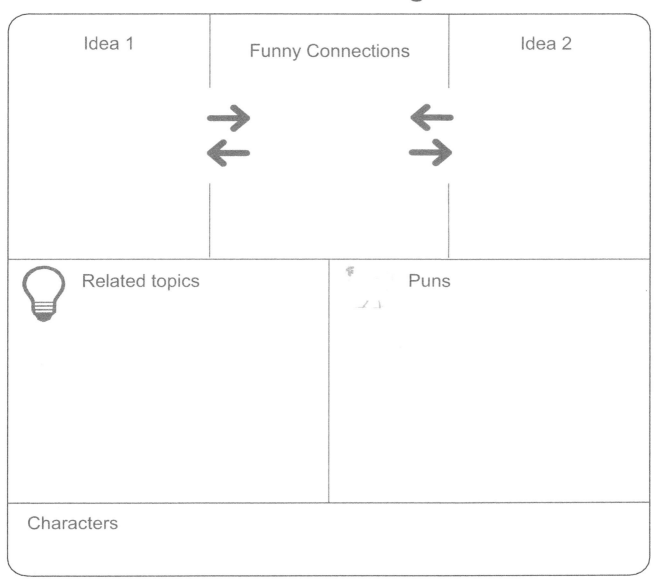

Idea 1	Funny Connections	Idea 2

Related topics

Puns

Characters

Joke

Setup

Punchline

Brainstorming

Idea 1	Funny Connections	Idea 2

💡 Related topics

Puns

Characters

Joke

Setup

Punchline

Brainstorming

Idea 1	Funny Connections	Idea 2

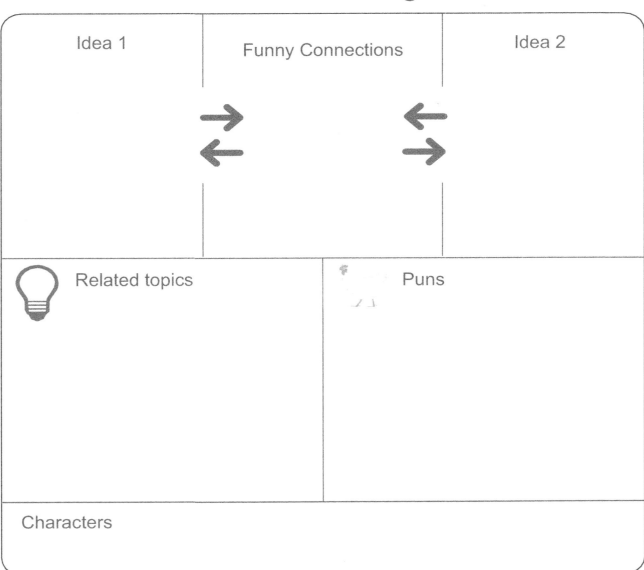

Related topics

Puns

Characters

Joke

Setup

Punchline

Brainstorming

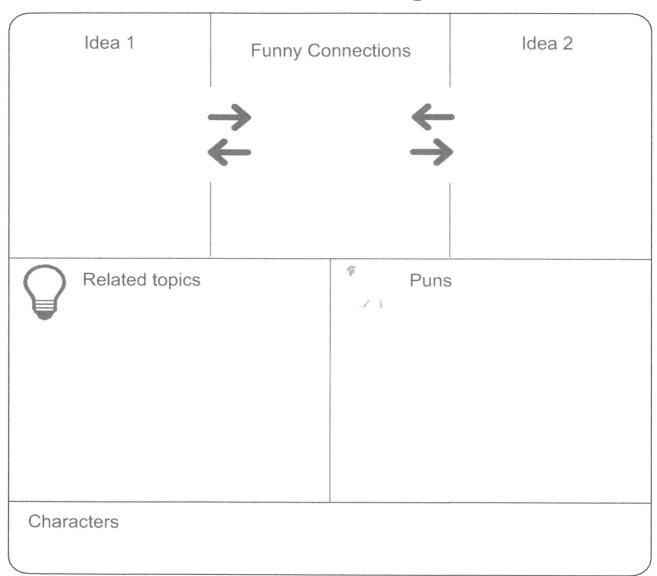

Idea 1	Funny Connections	Idea 2

Related topics

Puns

Characters

Joke

Setup

Punchline

Brainstorming

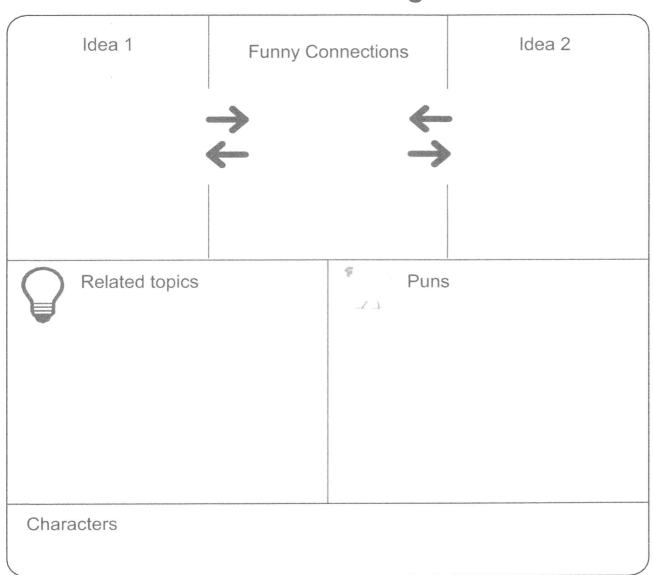

Idea 1	Funny Connections	Idea 2

Related topics

Puns

Characters

Joke

Setup

Punchline

Brainstorming

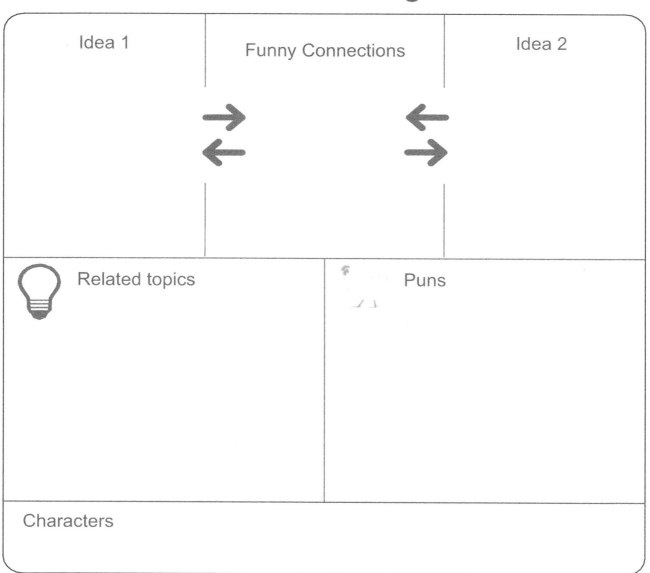

Idea 1	Funny Connections	Idea 2

Related topics

Puns

Characters

Joke

Setup

Punchline

Brainstorming

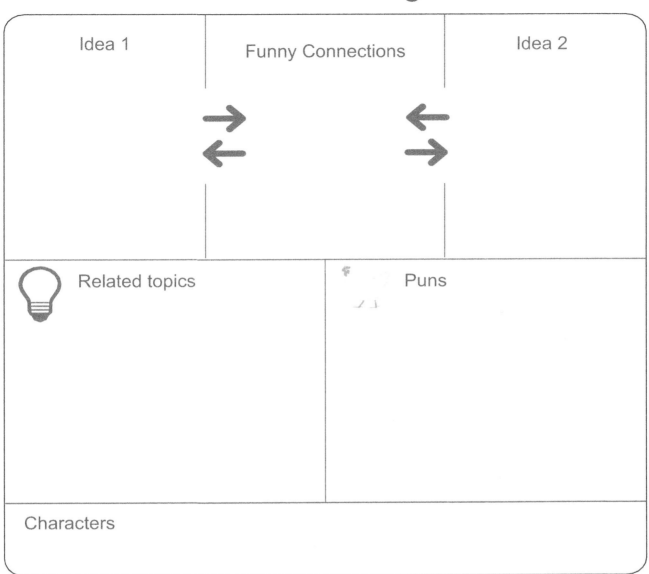

Idea 1	Funny Connections	Idea 2

Related topics

Puns

Characters

Joke

Setup

Punchline

Brainstorming

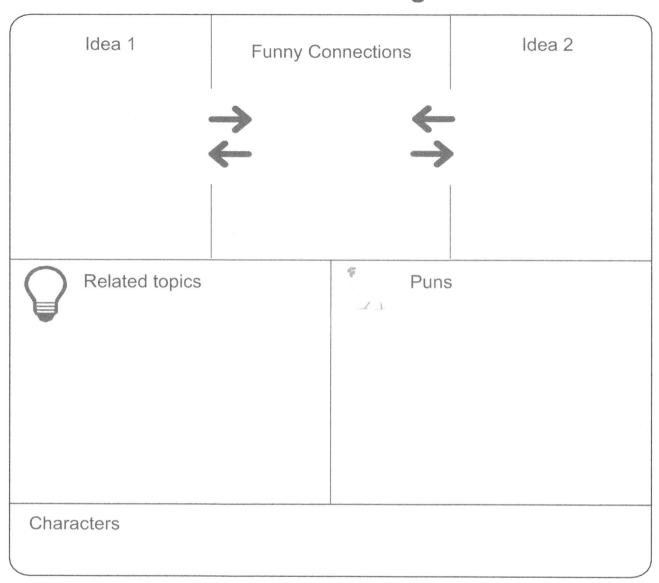

Idea 1	Funny Connections	Idea 2

Related topics

Puns

Characters

Joke

Setup

Punchline

Brainstorming

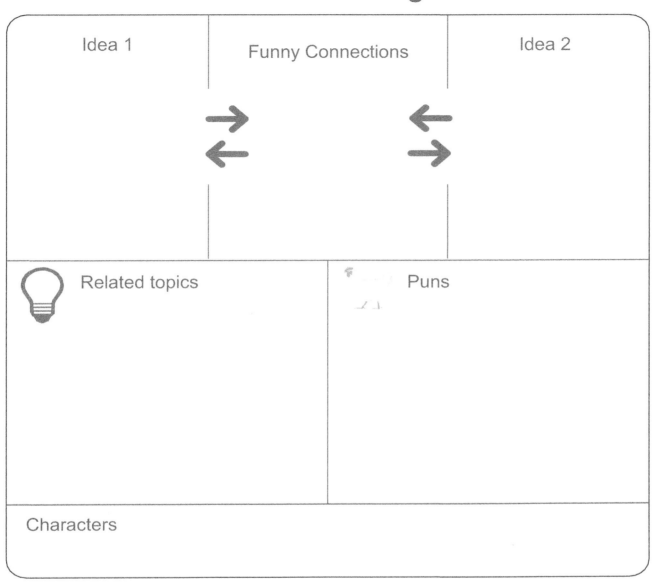

Idea 1

Funny Connections

Idea 2

Related topics

Puns

Characters

Joke

Setup

Punchline

Brainstorming

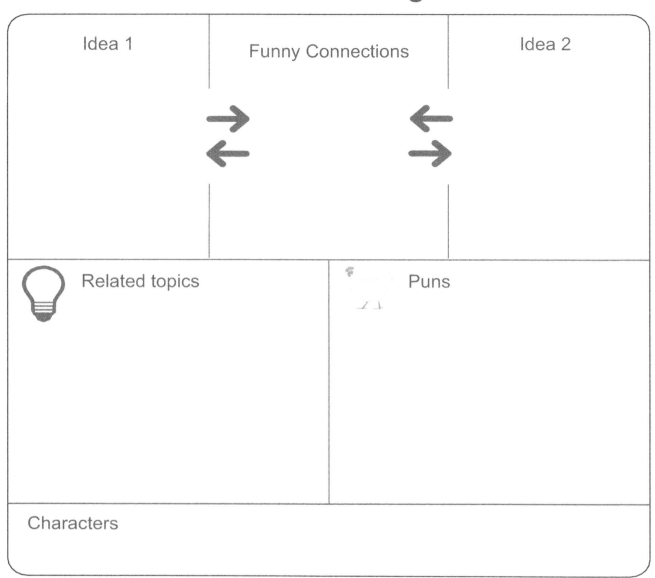

Idea 1	Funny Connections	Idea 2

Related topics

Puns

Characters

Joke

Setup

Punchline

Brainstorming

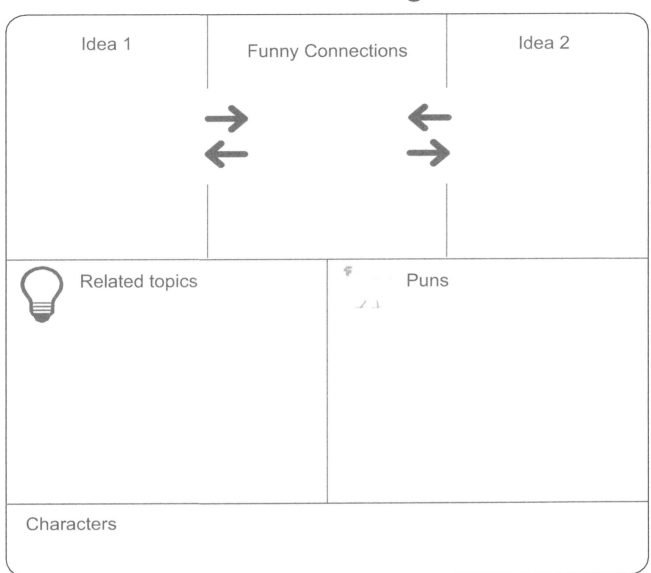

Idea 1	Funny Connections	Idea 2

Related topics

Puns

Characters

Joke

Setup

Punchline

Brainstorming

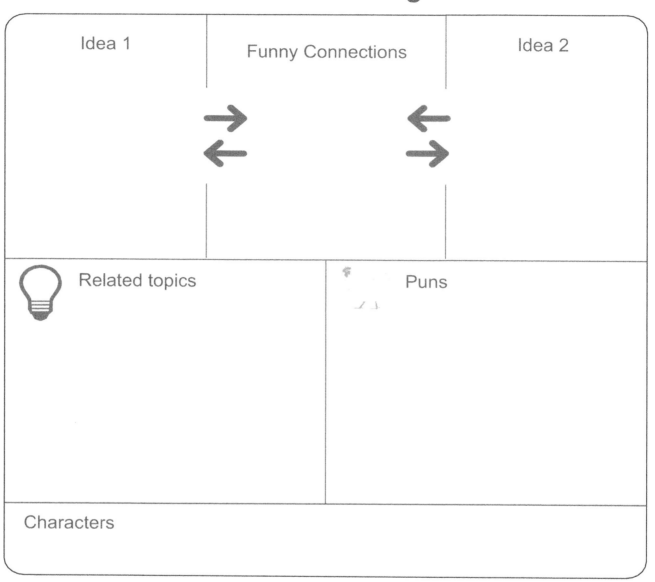

Idea 1	Funny Connections	Idea 2

Related topics

Puns

Characters

Joke

Setup

Punchline

Brainstorming

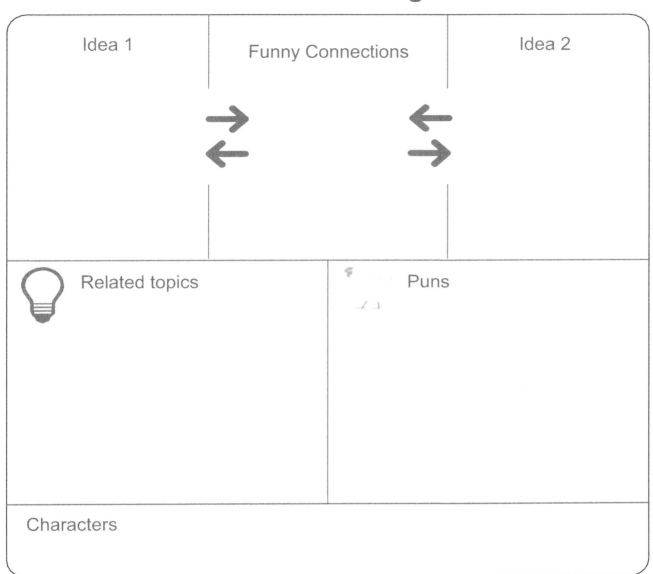

Idea 1	Funny Connections	Idea 2

Related topics

Puns

Characters

Joke

Setup

Punchline

Brainstorming

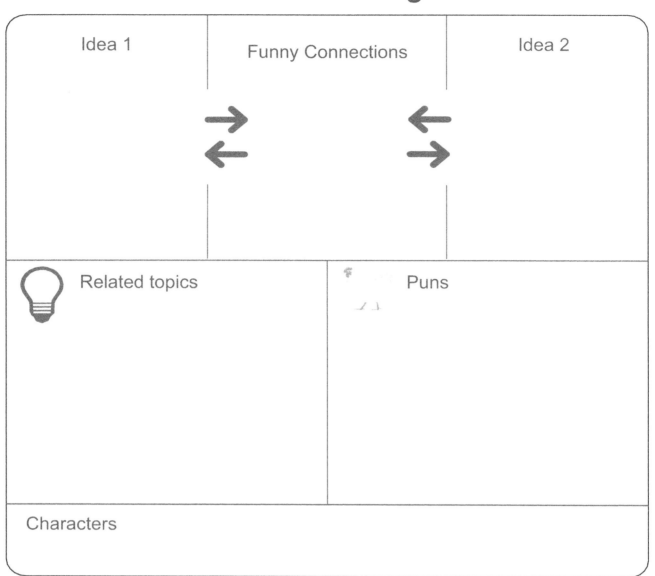

Idea 1	Funny Connections	Idea 2

Related topics

Puns

Characters

Joke

Setup

Punchline

Brainstorming

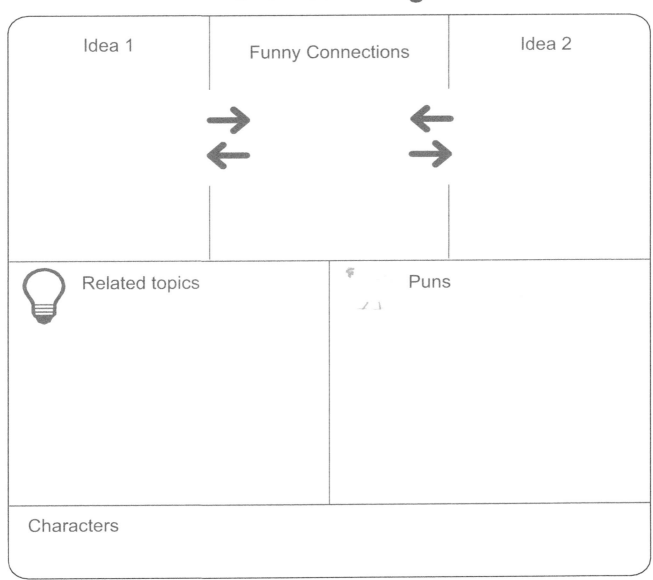

Idea 1	Funny Connections	Idea 2

💡 Related topics

Puns

Characters

Joke

Setup

Punchline

Brainstorming

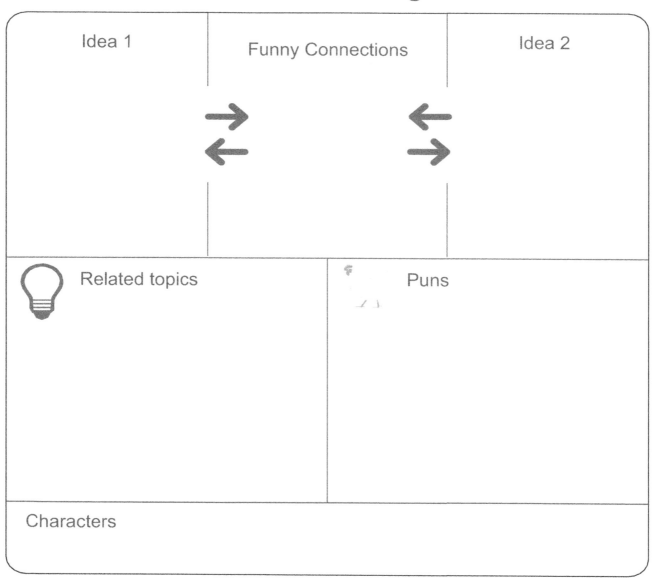

Idea 1	Funny Connections	Idea 2

Related topics

Puns

Characters

Joke

Setup

Punchline

Brainstorming

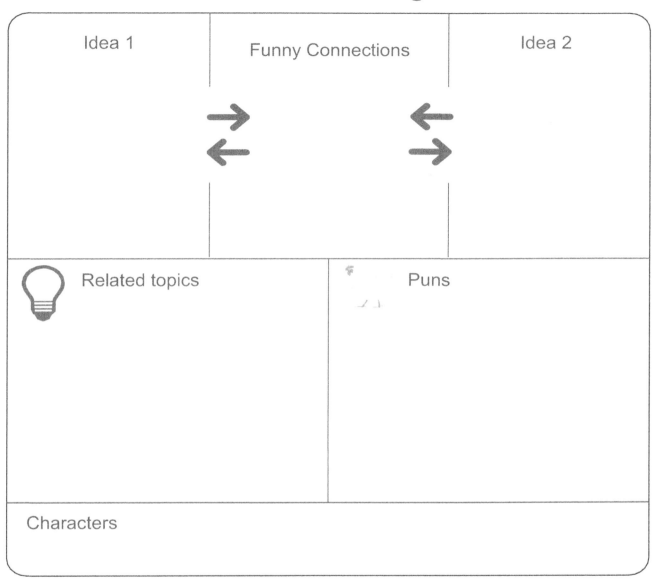

Idea 1	Funny Connections	Idea 2

Related topics

Puns

Characters

Joke

Setup

Punchline

Brainstorming

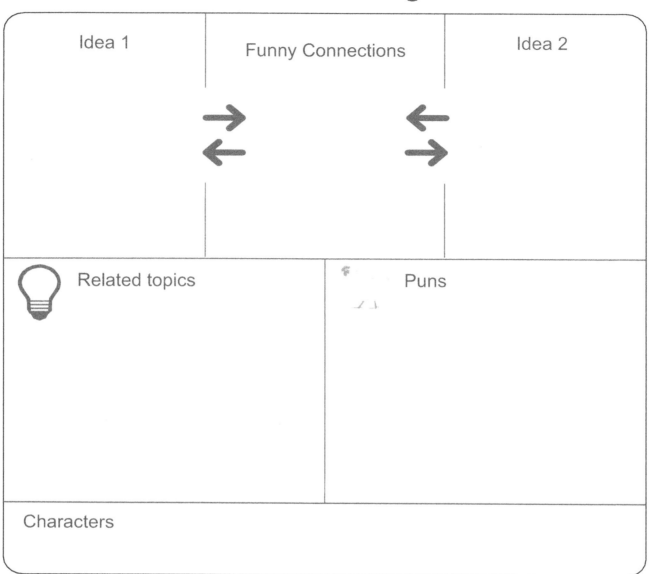

Idea 1	Funny Connections	Idea 2

Related topics	Puns

Characters

Joke

Setup

Punchline

Brainstorming

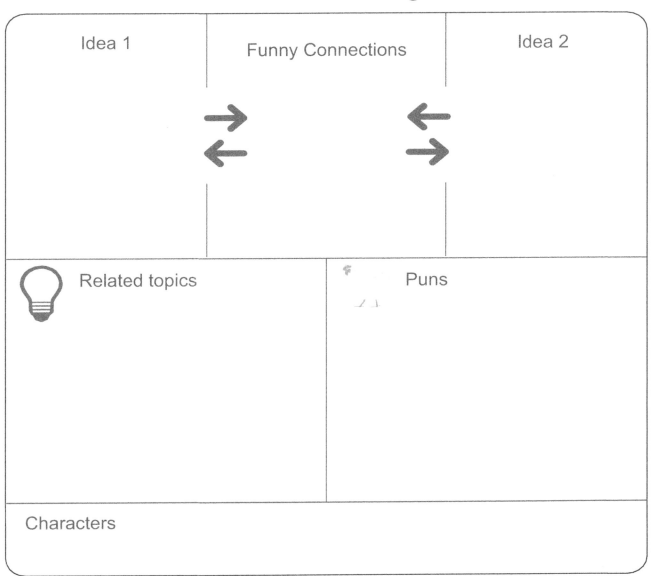

Idea 1	Funny Connections	Idea 2

Related topics

Puns

Characters

Joke

Setup

Punchline

Brainstorming

Idea 1	Funny Connections	Idea 2

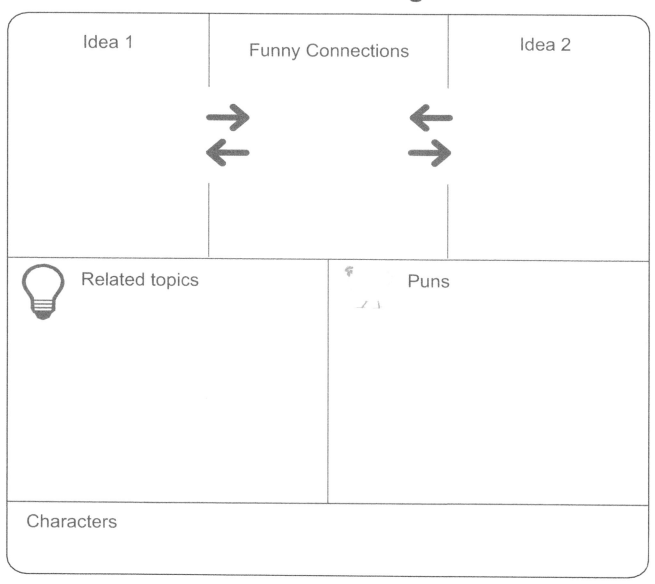

Related topics	Puns

Characters

Joke

Setup

Punchline

Brainstorming

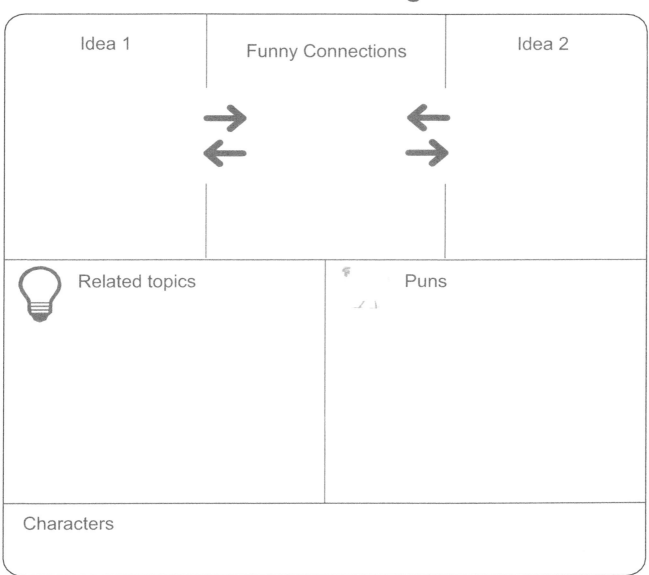

| | Idea 1 | Funny Connections | Idea 2 |

Related topics

Puns

Characters

Joke

Setup

Punchline

Brainstorming

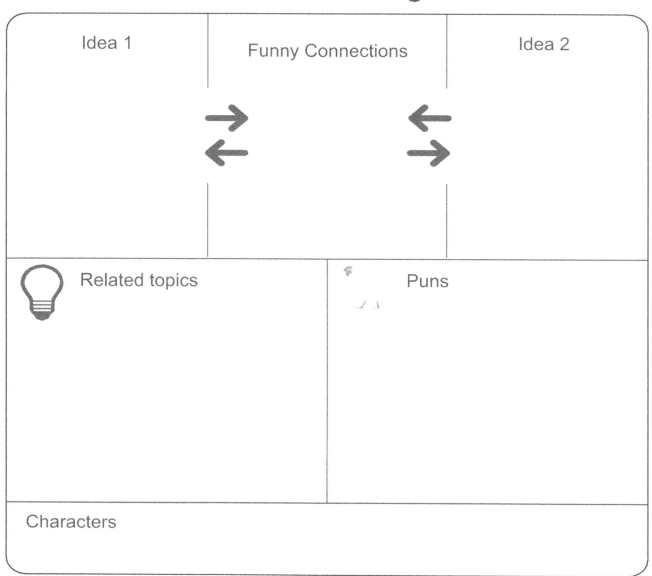

Idea 1	Funny Connections	Idea 2

Related topics

Puns

Characters

Joke

Setup

Punchline

Brainstorming

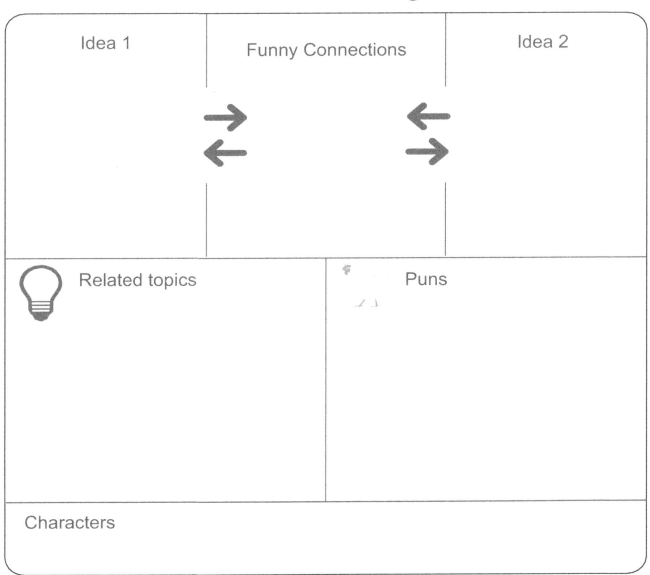

| | Idea 1 | Funny Connections | Idea 2 |

Related topics

Puns

Characters

Joke

Setup

Punchline

Made in the USA
Coppell, TX
06 January 2023

10523917R00070